MASTERING
PASTORAL
CARE

MASTERING
PASTORAL
CARE

Bruce Larson
Paul Anderson
Doug Self

MULTNOMAH

Portland, Oregon 97266

Christianity Today, Inc.

MASTERING PASTORAL CARE
© 1990 by Christianity Today, Inc.
Published by Multnomah Press
Portland, Oregon 97266

Multnomah Press is a ministry of Multnomah School of the Bible, 8435 N.E. Glisan Street, Portland, Oregon 97220.

Printed in the United States of America.

Library of Congress Cataloging-in-Publication Data

Larson, Bruce.
    Mastering pastoral care / Bruce Larson, Paul Anderson, Doug Self.
        p. cm.
    ISBN 0-88070-371-7
    1. Pastoral theology. 2. Clergy—Office I. Anderson, Paul, 1944-
II. Self, Doug.   III. Title.
BV4011.L37   1991
253—dc20   90-43237
                                                                              CIP

90 91 92 93 94 95 96 97 98 99 - 10 9 8 7 6 5 4 3 2 1

CONTENTS

Introduction   7
Mark Galli

Part 1
The Range of Pastoral Care

1. Home Visitation in an Age of Teleconferencing   15
   Doug Self

2. Letting the Laity Pastor   27
   Bruce Larson

3. Worship as Pastoral Care   37
   Paul Anderson

4. Ministering in the Marketplace   45
   Doug Self

Part 2
Special Concerns

5. Caring for Key Leaders   59
   Bruce Larson

6. Strategies for Ministering to Inactives   69
   Doug Self

7. Nurturing the Revitalized   85
   Paul Anderson

Part 3
Practicing Care

8. The Art of Pastoral Listening   97
   Doug Self

9. Risking Lay Ministry   109
   Bruce Larson

10. Using the Disciplines to Care   119
    Paul Anderson

11. Helping People Care for One Another   127
    Bruce Larson

12. Balancing Service and Solace   135
    Paul Anderson

    Epilogue   143
    Mark Galli

Introduction

Charles, our church organist, was scheduled for heart surgery — a quintuple bypass. Naturally I, his pastor, was concerned. So I went to see him the day before the operation. As I walked the hospital hallway to his room, I mentally rehearsed some well-worn psychology: no pious talk, elicit his fears, empathize with his anxiety.

"I imagine you're concerned about your operation," I said after some preliminary banter.

"Not particularly," he replied calmly.

Poor man is repressing, I thought. *If* I'm *worried about the operation, he certainly must be.* So I made a second stab.

"Oh, I'm sure the surgeon will do a fine job; he's got a good reputation. But still, the thought of someone working on one's heart unnerves most people."

"Well, I'm in God's hands. He will watch over me," he said, without a nervous twitch or pained expression. He seemed to have meant it.

I dropped the subject momentarily and let the conversation wander. *Maybe he needs to relax before he opens up*, I thought.

When it was time for me to go, I tried again, mumbling something about the seriousness of the operation.

"But God is good," he said as his glad eyes pierced me. "I'm confident God will be with me, no matter the outcome of the operation."

I stumbled through a prayer and walked out confused.

A few moments of reflection, however, revealed the source of my confusion. To begin with, Charles had more faith than I had imagined — certainly more confidence in God than I. But that wasn't the main thing.

Charles and I were also at odds about the purpose of my visit. I had come to dispense the comforts of modern psychology. Charles believed I should be there to give pastoral care. Charles was right.

It's not that modern psychology doesn't play a vital role in the administration of pastoral care. It's just that there's a spiritual dimension to pastoral care that the best psychology can only hint at. When Charles kept talking about God and kept insisting on faith, he reminded me of that simple truth.

Although we sometimes get distracted in an age saturated with Freud, Friedman, Maslow, and Rogers, most pastors know the truth Charles assumed. Without ignoring modern wise men, pastors are called to touch frazzled souls with the words of Matthew, Mark, Luke, and John.

But sometimes pastors are perplexed. They wonder how exactly to adapt modern wisdom to eternal ends. They wonder how to empathize with individuals, accepting them as they are, and yet guide them to new spiritual heights. They wonder how to give individual pastoral care to megacongregations. They wonder how to do home pastoral care for hectic people with cluttered calendars.

Three men who have so wondered have joined to write this volume of Mastering Ministry. They make no claim to have mastered pastoral care, but they have figured out some practical ways to make their spiritual care of people more effective.

Paul Anderson

Paul Anderson wants people to know the power and presence of the Spirit. And he's not afraid of prodding people to that end.

"I once phoned George, a member of the church," he told us, "to tell him I 'expected' to see him at the men's prayer group at six the following morning. Since he was not home, I left a message with his wife.

"My wife, who had heard me speaking on the phone, wondered why I had spoken so strongly and perhaps insensitively. The reason could be seen from what happened the next morning.

"When George's alarm went off, not so bright but early, he struggled to decide whether to get up. However, when his wife remembered my call and passed on my message, he immediately decided to come. Later, during the prayer meeting, George thanked the Lord for the 'encouragement' he had received from a brother who 'cared' that he came."

Paul took particular liberties with George because George was a coach and knew how to give and receive a challenge. So, although this isn't Paul's typical approach, it does illustrate his drive for people to know the exhilaration and life-shaping presence of the Holy Spirit. And that's also what characterizes his approach to pastoral care.

After graduating from Luther Theological Seminary in 1970, Paul joined the staff at Trinity Lutheran Church in San Pedro, California, eventually becoming senior pastor there in 1980. He has also written *Building Christian Character* (Bethany, 1980).

Doug Self

Doug Self wants members and visitors alike to know, at the earliest opportunity, the church cares. So he doesn't wait around for pastoral opportunities to happen. He visits people — in the home, at the job, on the sidewalk. And when he visits, he gives pastoral *care*.

He once described how he visits newcomers, for instance.

"I try to find out why they've come to church as well as what they don't like about church. I try to elicit the-church-did-this-to-me stories, because nearly everybody has one. The anger is often there, so it's best to get it out in the open, for them and for me.

"If people start talking about their resentments of the church, I don't get defensive. If they say, 'The church is always after money. Every time you sit down, they shove that offering plate under your nose,' I'll say, 'That's terrible! I hate it when churches do that. It makes me mad, too.' It so happens that we don't pass an offering plate at our church but have a box on the wall to receive donations.

"Whatever the resentment, however, I try to empathize with the sense of injustice or frustration. Once they see that I'm not interested in making them religious or churchy, they're more receptive to our church and the gospel."

Doug practices this type of pastoral care in two parishes in the Rocky Mountains of Colorado, one in Redstone and the other in Carbondale. He received an M.Div. from Southwestern Baptist Theological Seminary and a D.Min. from Denver Seminary. He has also edited *The Pastoral Care Newsletter*.

Bruce Larson

Bruce once described the genesis of his particular ministry emphasis:

"I was a student minister at a little church up on the Hudson River. I'd go up every weekend from Princeton, where I was in seminary. 'Fellowship' at that church consisted of a monthly meeting of the women's association and an occasional men's breakfast, where you had a baseball or football player give his testimony.

"Then one weekend, I found out some shocking news: a teenage girl in the congregation had left the community to live with her older brother. She was pregnant.

"I said to the woman who told me, 'Could I go see her?'

" 'Oh, no,' she replied. 'You're the *last* person she wants to know what's happened.'

"Suddenly it hit me: *That's what's wrong with the church in our time. It's the place where you wear only your best clothes; you sit in Sunday school, you worship, you have a potluck together, but you don't bring your life! You leave behind all your pain, your brokenness, your hopes, even your joys.*"

That the church in the nineties largely is no longer like that is due in part to the ministry of Bruce Larson. After that experience, Bruce developed his ideas about honesty, sharing, and the role of small groups in nurturing Christians. Today, *small groups* and *Bruce Larson* are synonymous to many. In this book, Bruce reminds us that small groups are the perfect complement to a pastor's ministry, since they allow lay people to perform pastoral care with one another and in ways a pastor cannot.

A graduate of Princeton Theological Seminary, Bruce has pastored churches in New York, Illinois, and Washington. He presently serves as co-pastor at the Crystal Cathedral in Garden Grove, California. He has also served as president of Faith at Work and written over twenty books, including *The Presence: The God Who Delivers and Guides* (Harper & Row, 1988).

Practical Concern for Real People

You've probably gathered that these three authors approach pastoral care in three significantly different ways. They have different goals as well as different means. Pastoral care doesn't fall into any dreary stereotype.

Nonetheless, these men share a common outlook on pastoral care: it is, first and foremost, practical concern for the spiritual lives of individuals. That common vision is what unites this book.

One caveat is in order. Much of pastoral care is done in

confidence. Yet in order for our authors to illustrate their points effectively, we've asked them to include detailed examples from their ministries. Consequently, and more so than in other volumes of Mastering Ministry, names, gender, and circumstances have often been changed to protect pastoral confidentiality.

What hasn't changed, of course, is the reality behind the confidentiality: real people receiving genuine pastoral care. And that, we trust, will spur you on to mastering pastoral care, no matter how you do it.

— Mark Galli
associate editor, LEADERSHIP
Carol Stream, Illinois

PART ONE

The Range of Pastoral Care

Home visitation is an awesome opportunity and respon-
sibility. For many people, I can be an extension of Christ,
an expression, albeit imperfect, of God's love.

— Doug Self

CHAPTER ONE

Home Visitation in an Age of Teleconferencing

A typical day of pastoral visitation:

Early in the afternoon, I visited a blended family. The wife had a child from a previous live-in; the husband had children from a previous marriage. They were desperately trying to blend the families together. It didn't take long to get down to business. They were troubled that, because of the tension in the family, one of the husband's children had left to live with the husband's former wife. To make matters worse, the husband had just lost his job. The family was pummeled and hurting.

Although the joblessness was new, the knotty problem with the children was not. There weren't any easy answers. We analyzed a recent family blowup to search for better ways to handle their conflicts. Although I didn't want to lecture them, I did try to help them trust God in the midst of their turmoil.

As I got ready to leave, the husband, the wife, and I joined hands in prayer. I asked God to put his arms around these two bewildered and exhausted Christians.

A short time later, I was visiting a young couple who had been attending our church for a few Sundays. What a joy! They had recently moved to our community and had been invited by some regular attenders. During our visit they assured me they'd found their church home with us. I love to hear new people excitedly describe what they've found meaningful about our church.

At the last stop of the day, I counseled a soon-to-be-wed couple. The prospective bride had a child from a previous marriage and was now six months pregnant. The prospective groom told me how disappointed he was over losing several previous children with other women. One child lived a week, and three others were miscarried because of the women's drug use.

I thought to myself, *How can the world get so messed up?* The two were wandering around in life, trying to put something together. They hadn't been significantly touched by the church, yet they called on me to perform their ceremony. So I tried to use that opportunity to build a relationship, and I hope to see them trust in Christ eventually.

Visitation: At the Heart of Ministry

Every pastor has strengths, gifts, and interests. Some may emphasize preaching, others administration, others teaching.

For me, visitation has become the joy and strength of my ministry. Some days visiting is an adventure; other days it's drudgery. But my pastoral ministry cannot exist without it.

Not all pastors, of course, will make visitation their top priority. Nonetheless, personal care for members remains a vital part of every pastor's ministry for three reasons.

- *It's central to our call.* To some degree, the words we use to describe our calling determine the nature of that calling. We call ourselves *ministers,* so we serve our people. We call ourselves *preachers,* so we proclaim God's Word. If we call ourselves *pastors,* that means we will also shepherd the church flock.

As a shepherd is responsible for the sheep, being with people is the heart of the pastor's responsibilities. In his book, *Pastoral Theology,* Thomas C. Oden, professor of theology at Drew University, says, "The pastoral office is by definition a shepherding task. . . . Shepherding cannot be done at a sterile distance, with automated telephone answering services, computerized messages, and impersonal form letters. By definition there cannot be an absentee shepherd. There can be no mail-order or mechanized pastoral service, because pastoring is personal. It is not just public talk but interpersonal meeting where richer self-disclosures are possible."

On one of my visits to a schoolteacher in our community, she told me of a child in her school. The child's mother is twice divorced. While the child was visiting her father in another state, the mother moved in with a new boyfriend and his parents. One morning after the child returned, the mother and boyfriend fought, and the little girl assumed the blame for it. She was brokenhearted, feeling out of place in a strange house.

I grieved for the child and admired the teacher, with whom I then prayed. I didn't preach or evangelize; I didn't administrate, delegate, or plan. But I performed essential Christian ministry: I spent time with a member of my congregation, learned from her experience, and encouraged her in her faith.

- *People need pastoral contact.* Those who analyze our culture and business world underscore the value of personal contact for leaders. John Naisbitt in his book *Megatrends* says that in a high-tech society people crave high touch. Peters and Waterman in their book *In Search of Excellence* emphasize the importance of MBWA, Management by Walking Around. Effective management happens best through personal contact, the personal touch.

Likewise in the church, a recent survey summarized in the

Ministerial Competency Report shows that lay people consistently thought pastoral calling important, even more than ministers did.

I've found that routine pastoral calls, during which we don't talk about anything urgent, are the most important ones to church members. Such contacts say clearly, "Your pastor cares for you — not just about spiritual things, but about you."

Recently, during our church's anniversary celebration, folks noted what they appreciated about our church. One man wrote, "A pastor who takes time with his flock, to lift them up out of the stony places, to encourage, to uphold in prayer on a continuing basis." People need pastoral contact.

- *It's a primary way to love incarnationally.* As one minister put it, "Pastoral visitation is incarnational: the Word became flesh and visited among us."

I regularly call on a grandmother who lives with one of her daughters. The older woman's husband divorced her years ago, leaving her to raise the children, including one handicapped child. Her grown sons got into drugs. Her married son and his wife neglect their children. She also dislikes her job and feels detached from her community because she and her daughter have had to move several times over the years. I always feel her anguish.

The grandmother is powerless to do anything except love and pray. Many times she is heartsick and weary. Yet I stand in awe of her, as does the community and church, because she's also a model of strength and integrity.

Before I leave, we join hands for prayer, and I usually pray that God will embrace her with love and strength. Yet somehow I feel that, as her pastor, I'm one who can literally embrace her. Most members don't have the time or ability to visit her. I do. It's an awesome opportunity and responsibility, but I feel that for many people like her, I can be an extension of Christ for them, an expression, albeit imperfect, of God's love.

Misconceptions Reconceived

We can line up the witnesses for visitation's defense — professors, business consultants, even the Bible — yet it continues to be dreaded or neglected by many pastors. That's partly due to bad experiences. But sometimes it's due to misconceptions. In particular, three misconceptions need to be cleared up.

1. Visitation is an inefficient use of time. With so many to minister to, the pastor may feel that time spent with individuals is not as effective as time spent with a group. That's not necessarily so.

I once read an article in an advertising journal that explained a hierarchy of communication effectiveness. The least effective method for influencing people's attitudes, it said, was mass advertising — newspaper or the TV. The article progressed up a half-dozen steps to describe finally the most effective method: personal time with an individual.

A well-timed conversation with an unchurched person or a growing member, then, can be the most effective time I spend. In a personal conversation, a pastor can respond to another's specific situation.

Mr. Kilmer was my fifth grade teacher. He was popular at Eugene Field Elementary School; all the kids wanted to be in his class. No wonder: he spent time with kids. I still remember the Saturday afternoon Mr. Kilmer invited me to his house to watch baseball on TV with him and his family. Wow, was I impressed! And I was more apt to attend to his lessons after that.

2. Visitation is too difficult to schedule. Even though I live and pastor in the mountains near Aspen, Colorado, life speeds by at a hectic pace. Some people here drive half an hour or more to work; others work late shifts at the coal mine. Who knows when they'll be home or in bed grabbing a few winks?

In the summer people enjoy the great outdoors, hiking, driving a jeep through the mountains, or gathering wood for the winter. During winter they're either skiing or recuperating from the icy drive home through a blizzard. People like to get cozy and relax in front of the hearth. They're not looking to be disturbed.

So, everyone is busy these days, even laid-back country folks. It may be difficult to schedule visits in the home, but that doesn't mean it's impossible, or unimportant. I've found visitation powerfully enhances ministry and our church's health. So, I put up with some of the obstacles and try to overcome others.

Each week I schedule several afternoons and evenings for visitation. I have to pace myself, of course. Mornings, Tuesday through Saturday, are my study times. At noon I jog and shower. Especially if I'm going to go calling, I rest and relax a few hours in the afternoon, spending time with my family. Around 3 P.M., several afternoons a week, I head out to see people.

Sometimes I have appointments, but mostly I just drop by. I've been around long enough to know family schedules — work shifts, dinner time, bed time. Naturally, I try to work my visits around their schedules. In addition, people are used to me dropping in, especially afternoons and evenings. We all accept the awkwardness that visitation sometimes entails because we know the difference it makes.

3. *Visitation is risky and scary.* Facing individuals on their home turf can be unnerving. However, dreading pastoral visitation is not a 1990's development. Early in this century, J. H. Jowett dealt with the pastor's home calling in one of his Yale lectures on preaching:

"The difficulty of delivering a message is in inverse proportion to the size of the audience. To face the individual soul with the Word of God . . . is one of the heaviest commissions given to our charge. Where there are ten men who can face a crowd, there is only one who can face the individual. Gentlemen, it seemed as though I could preach a sermon and never meet a devil. But as soon as I began to take my sermon to the individual, the streets were thick with devils" (*The Preacher, His Life and Work*).

This anxiety is aggravated if a pastor thinks poorly of himself or fears rejection. The pastor may fear that professional credibility may be seriously jeopardized in personal conversation. People might ask tough questions about spiritual matters. Someone might have a grudge against the church or Christianity and find the visiting pastor a convenient target.

There's another side to this experience, however. Certainly, some of my most uncomfortable moments in the pastorate have come in a family's living room. But I've also had unique opportunities to minister to people directly, immediately, personally.

Once, when I visited a family who attends our church occasionally, I happened into a argument. As I was sitting in the living room, visiting with the mother and father, the teenage son came home. He walked through the living room, threw a casual greeting over his shoulder, and went to his room. Suddenly he stormed back into the living room and demanded, "What happened to my room?"

The mother's anger overrode her desire to keep up appearances. "I told you this morning to clean up your room, but you just sat around and listened to your music and then rushed off to school," she stormed.

"But you didn't have to pile all my clothes in the middle of the room!"

"You haven't washed your clothes for a month, so I just put them where you could see them!"

The son stomped off to his room and slammed the door to punctuate his exit. As the father and I looked at each other, he shifted uncomfortably. We began to talk about family conflict. Needless to say, they were eager to hear some biblical insight into family living.

I've been put on the spot to explain why a good God can allow evil to exist. I've been that convenient target for people fed up with the church. Sometimes after a difficult experience, I've crawled home feeling whipped, a failure.

But I've also matured through those experiences, and I've been able to turn many of those awkward moments into growing experiences for others. In sports they say, "No pain, no gain." In the pastorate, I'd put it more positively: with pain comes much gain.

Visitation Builds Better Ministry

Haddon Robinson talks about the "halo effect" in ministry, the extraordinary regard church members sometimes accord their preacher, and the positive effect it has on ministry. One factor that contributes to the halo effect is the deepening relationship between pastor and people, especially as the pastor visits people through the years.

Let me show specifically how pastoral visitation has enhanced my ministry.

● *Preaching is enriched.* Many pastors put in long hours to study the Word. But I've found my preaching is better still if I also invest myself in a thorough study of my people. Pastoral visitation gives me a handle on the questions people are asking and the issues they are facing.

Bob wanted to get together because he was in a quandary about a new job opportunity. I'd known Bob and his wife for a couple of years. He was likable, enthusiastic and well-meaning. But he was obviously agitated as we began our talk.

"He avoids talking and thinking about it," said his wife, Peg. "He'll work on a thousand-piece puzzle and rent an armload of videos before talking about it."

"I'm scared," Bob added. "I'm afraid of making a wrong decision. I see things as either right or wrong, black or white. But I don't know which is the right choice. Why can't God let me know unmistakably?"

"So, how do you usually make decisions?" I asked.

"I'm usually ready to do it when an idea first comes up. I often volunteer for things. But later I begin to have doubts: *Should I do it or should I back out?* I hate that, so I put off decisions as long as I can."

Bob and I then talked about a subject we had discussed before: his boyhood relationship with his father. His father had been quick to hand out orders but not to give praise. His father always found something wrong with the work Bob had done. Instead of saying, "Nice job" after Bob shoveled the walk, for example, his father would say, "Come on, Bob. The shovel hangs on the wall. Can't you do anything right?"

As we talked, slowly he made some breakthroughs. He was finally able to see that God loves him in spite of decisions.

Many people struggle with decisions as does Bob, and many

times the root of their struggle lies in childhood. With Bob's permission, I preached a message that surfaced such issues. It touched a cord; many were in tears by the end.

"One of the most palpable benefits that most pastors will realize from visitation," writes Thomas Oden, "is the kindling of the homiletical mind. Let us assume that due confidentiality will be maintained. Pastoral conversation will furnish the mind of the preacher with a pregnant train of ideas and kernels of insight. Biblical subjects will be animated by rich experiential vitality" (*Pastoral Theology*).

● *Administration is made easier.* If the pastor develops a feel for people's spiritual states, the church's ministry program can be more accurately and sensitively planned.

Several weeks ago I counseled with a young couple, Martin and Connie. Their problems were many: they hadn't spent time alone together in months, their preschool children were demanding more attention, money was tight, and each was ready to walk out on the other.

We talked for a while, and then I left. My heart went out to them, but I recognized they were not alone. Indeed it was the problem of many young families. How could our church help?

As I thought and prayed, I finally came up with an idea: What if we matched up a younger family with a family whose children were older or gone from the home?

During the next Sunday's morning service, I left the pulpit and walked down the center aisle. I began talking about the pressures that families with young children face day in and day out. I suggested the idea of a family with older children adopting the younger family for support, encouragement, and childcare a couple of times a month. Applause broke out.

I continued walking toward the back of the auditorium where Martin and Connie were sitting. Having gotten their permission ahead of time, I introduced them to our congregation (they were newcomers) and asked for a volunteer family to be "grandparents," "aunts," or "uncles."

For a moment no one moved. Then Tom Hammond raised his

hand. Tom and his wife, Dee, are middle-aged with several children, almost all grown.

The congregation was buzzing after the service about the idea. Martin told me several people approached them after the service and offered assistance. Visitation, then, led to a church program targeted to meet genuine needs.

• *Crises are averted.* By continual circulation, dropping in from time to time, I often can detect a crisis in the making. It might be that seeds of conflict, explosive anger, or despair lie just below the surface. Often, through an extended time of personal ministry, I can help a person can get a grip on the problem.

Once when I visited Sally, a woman I had counseled often over the years, she told me about the latest troubles of her daughter and son-in-law. Mac and Ginny's several years of marriage had been marked by fights, drinking, and misery, although for some reason they stayed together.

They weren't interested in coming to church, and they wouldn't listen to anyone. They weighed heavily on Sally's heart. Often she was drawn into their lives, getting caught between fighting parents and feeling she had to rescue their baby during a night of drinking and arguing.

When she was through explaining the latest episodes, she said, "I know there's nothing anyone can do, but it's frustrating. I feel so alone with this problem."

"No, there's no one who can actually solve the problem," I responded. "But there are some friends who could help you bear the problem, some friends who could listen, understand, and pray with you about it."

She appeared puzzled momentarily. "That would help. But I just hate to keep talking about it. Year after year, there's no improvement. My friends would get tired of me moaning about it and desert me."

"Maybe there are a few special friends, some friends whom you've walked with in their difficulties. There's Sherry, and Molly. I know they think the world of you."

"I guess you're right, Doug," she replied. "They do know

some of what's going on with Mac and Ginny. But I don't think they really know how it's affecting me. But I don't want to be a burden to anyone."

"As far as I'm concerned, you're not a burden; you're a friend. Believe me, I know that there are a lot of people in the church who would feel as I do."

That conversation was pivotal for Sally. She had been discouraged about Mac and Ginny, feeling increasingly isolated. Aside from providing the suggestion that she talk with friends, the pastoral visit alone averted a crisis of deepening depression.

● *Ministry is affirmed.* An effective pastoral visitation ministry can give the pastor a sense of accomplishment. Pastors work with a lot of intangibles. Often success or failure is measured by an ill-timed comment mumbled by a disgruntled member on his way out of the Sunday service. Let's face it: pastors could do with a regular dose of satisfaction and achievement.

I'd known George and Maggie for nearly ten years. I'd sat with them in my study and in their living room on numerous occasions.

However, George, while warm, had always held me at arm's length. While Maggie had attended church regularly with the kids for eight years, George found something else to do on Sundays. He acknowledged his intention to develop his relationship with Christ, but he did little about it.

Then he began been facing some business problems that weren't yielding to his usual efficiency. And business stress was adversely affecting his family life. Although I knew about his problems, on this night I had just happened to stop by on a routine pastoral call, intending no more than a friendly visit.

After greeting me warmly, George quickly plunged into describing his frustrations. I empathized with him about his pain and confusion.

When it seemed appropriate, I mentioned that at certain crisis points it's helpful to step back and consider the whole of life. Once in a while a man must ask hard questions such as, "What am I living for?" "What am I accomplishing?" "Am I investing my energies in what will bring a deep sense of accomplishment?"

George had been asking himself just those questions, so he was eager for wisdom. I suggested some ways he might effectively analyze his problems — spiritual, vocational, and marital. My words fell like rain on parched earth. Sometimes his face brightened; other himes his brow furrowed, indicating deep thought. He commented several times that he wished he had his tape recorder running so he could save the conversation.

He then talked about his wife. He acknowledged that her life of constancy had been an inspiration to him. Her deeper relationship with the Lord had impressed and attracted him. As a result, he felt he could now more readily give himself to Christ. His wife was beaming and crying. Her prayers of many years were being answered.

We prayed together; we wept together. As I left, George squared his shoulders, gave me a firm handshake, and said, "Doug, you'll never know how much you've meant to us. Your coming by tonight was perfect timing. I needed what you had to say. I'm ready to get serious with God. It's time. Thanks."

One by One, Day In and Day Out

Pastoral visiting offers great variety, as the examples from this chapter illustrate. In fact, the pastor must be able to read family situations as quickly as an NFL quarterback reads defenses.

Yet for all the skill required, visitation isn't nearly as glamorous as professional sports. Directors don't make movies or TV shows about routine pastoral visitation. There are no songs immortalizing it.

But maybe there ought to be, because pastors across the world put in five to twenty hours a week visiting the people in their churches and communities. They gently teach. They give assurance. They offer prayers. They keep families together. They comfort the grieving. They rejoice with the joyful. In their words and especially with their presence, they communicate to an increasingly impersonal world of mass media and teleconferencing that God cares for individuals, one by one, day in and day out.

The best measure of a church is how many people walk out to be the royal priesthood on Monday and Tuesday and Wednesday. The basic product of the church is people in ministry.

— Bruce Larson

CHAPTER TWO

Letting the Laity Pastor

I had a chance to meet Donald Peterson just before he retired as chairman of Ford Motor Company. He'd been chairman when Ford ebbed to its lowest point economically and also when the company had turned around and reached its apex. "How do you account for what happened?" I asked him. "Was it robots, mechanization?"

"No," he said, "it was two less tangible things. First, we redefined our goal. We said our goal was to build a car free of construction errors. Second, we gave our people the power to build it. We gave all our workers the authority to stop the line whenever they found something wrong. When we did that, we went from an average of forty-seven flaws per car to one flaw in every two cars."

The key to renewing Ford Motor Company was getting back to basics — building a flawless car. In much the same way, pastoral care for church members begins when the congregation is brought back to its basic mission.

What is the bottom line for the church, the true measure of its success?

Some churches measure success by buildings, size, staff, budget, or how many missionaries they support. Some churches inspire, inform, and educate. All that is fine. But to me the church is not primarily an institution and not primarily in the inspiration business or the information business or the education business. Great sermons or fine buildings don't matter if the church isn't becoming a kingdom of priests.

In the Old Testament, God chastised his people because they refused to be priests. The best measure of a church is how many people walk out to be the royal priesthood on Monday and Tuesday and Wednesday. To me, then, the basic product of the church is *people in ministry.*

Unlike Ford's product, the church's product cannot be precisely measured. But keeping that goal clear remains crucial for me. People in ministry becomes the goal of our worship and education.

And people in ministry becomes the measure especially of pastoral care. Pastoral care includes visiting the sick, weeping with the grieving, praying with the concerned. But to me its ultimate purpose is to get lay people involved in ministry to one another and to the world. Pastoral care is not just care done by the pastor but care given in a pastoral way by anyone. People involved in ministry, then, is not only a goal of my pastoral care but also the way my pastoral care is broadened geometrically.

What Is Ministry?

If people in ministry is the true measure of the church, then we need to define ministry. When I did a Bible study of "ministry," I found more models than I expected.

• For the servant girl who spoke to her master, Naaman, ministry was simply bearing witness: "There is a place where God does business where you can get healed."

• Elijah's greatest ministry was to disciple Elisha: "Come join me. I won't be around long. Learn what I know. Do what I do."

• Mary and Martha had a retreat-center ministry. Jesus could come to their home and take off his sandals and eat matzo ball soup and enjoy the company of two women and their brother, Lazarus.

• Then there's the ministry of Lydia who opened her home, which became a strategic center as the first Christian church in Europe.

• Priscilla and Aquila were two lay people who dared to take on the training of Apollos, a gifted preacher, and say, "Do you understand the theology? We think we can help you improve your ministry." I saw the same thing happen in a former church of mine, where for years the people trained their pastors to be better pastors.

All these biblical examples of ministry have at least one thing in common: they show that lay people did — and can do — every one of them.

Barriers to Ministry

If none of these kinds of ministry takes professional training, if lay people can do them, then why don't we find more lay people ministering? I think there are a couple of reasons.

One barrier to lay ministry is the feeling of inadequacy. We tend to feel that only those with great wisdom, knowledge, and skill can heal and bless and release people. We think, *Who am I? I'm no Mother Teresa, no Saint Paul!*

We may feel we're being humble, but it's really a way to avoid responsibility. Those who put the professional on a pedestal are at the same time relieving themselves of any involvement in ministry. They ask, "Why isn't the church (meaning the pastor) doing something about this person or that situation?"

To say "I'm only a lay person; I'm not worthy" is copping out. Who *is* worthy? God says, "Do it!"

Fear of failure raises another barrier to lay ministry. What if I pray with somebody and there are no visible results? I'm sure that occurred often in the New Testament era, too, but only the miracles were recorded. I once heard Oral Roberts say, "Nobody has ever experienced more unanswered prayers for healing than I have." We don't always see immediate answers to our prayers.

When we first started healing services at University Presbyterian Church in Seattle, some of our elders were uneasy. We worked in groups of three — one pastor and two elders — and people came forward and sought prayer for physical and mental healing, relationships, and addictions. When we prayed, we knew there would be miracles, but we couldn't say where or when or how.

As time passed, the elders were feeling more secure in praying for healing. They were learning not to be afraid of what looked like a failure, because they realized that prayer is never wasted. Even when we can't see results, God is at work.

So how do we launch inadequate-feeling and fearful people into ministry? The key is to convince them that ministry doesn't mean having the answers. In fact, coming up with pat answers usually is the worst approach. However, when we minister from weakness, not knowing what answers are needed but actively listening, we model for them the ministry we'd like them to engage in.

Four Kinds of Ministry

I divide ministry into four distinct kinds.

First, there's *material ministry.* That involves giving money and goods to bless and heal and help people. Material ministry might be digging wells in Haiti or building a church in Latin America or painting a shelter for battered women. It's people providing material goods for others.

For example, two retired executive women had a special concern for the down-and-out on Seattle's skid row. One night a week, these women took sandwich fixings to the First Avenue Service Center, where they made sandwiches while dispensing care and conversation to the street people seeking food. Over the years they have dispensed a lot of love and dignity as well as more than a million sandwiches.

Junior high students in that same parish engaged in what they called "Midnight Marauder" activities. No, it wasn't vandalism. The Midnight Marauders were squads of junior highers who delivered surprise dinners to single working parents. For example, they would place a couple of hot pizzas on the doorstep, ring the bell, and run like crazy. The single parent, tired from a full day at work, would open the door to find dinner and a note saying, "The Midnight Marauders have struck again!" The recipients were understandably touched that someone understood their burdens.

Second, there is *spiritual ministry* — introducing people to Jesus Christ and to life in the Spirit.

Our churches, unfortunately, are full of unconverted believers, who ascribe to all the right doctrines but don't allow those beliefs to impact their lives. They need to move into a vital relationship with the God they believe in. A small group is one way of moving these people toward that goal.

I can think of one woman in particular, a deeply unhappy woman who over a ten-year period endured assorted illnesses and even underwent organ transplants. Although she was only 40, she was already frail. The final blow came when her husband divorced her. When that happened, I thought she might die.

However, she was part of a small group, and when he left her, that group of ordinary Christians ministered to her in many ways. They helped her come to grips with how she would handle life with her husband gone. They encouraged her to return to school to obtain job skills. She got her driver's license and became more independent. Increasingly, by means of this group, the Lord moved into her life, and I watched her become a new person.

Obviously, spiritual ministry takes place on a one-to-one basis, as well. We can do that by example, certainly, but during *kairos* times we can speak of life and truth to another in need and introduce people to our Lord, Redeemer, and Friend.

Third, there is *healing ministry*, or more broadly, wholeness ministry. This includes helping people become medically, mentally, physically, and emotionally whole. After he raised Lazarus from the dead, Jesus told those standing by to unwrap him. There are countless church members who have been raised from the dead but have never been unwrapped. They're alive and walking, but they're still bound with fear and guilt. Jesus gives them new life, and it is our job to unwrap them.

A doctor I know told about one of his elderly patients who was suddenly gripped with severe rheumatoid arthritis. When he examined her, her hands were like claws. Trying to understand her sudden affliction, he asked her, almost casually, "Has anything been happening in your life lately?"

"I know exactly what you mean, Doctor," she replied coldly, "and furthermore, I have no intention of forgiving him!"

Obviously, the physician had uncovered the problem that was producing the symptoms. So many of our mental and even physical problems are rooted in our attitudes.

Glen Warner, a Seattle oncologist, practices a whole-person medicine. He uses traditional chemotherapy and radiation treatments for cancer, but his immunotherapy operates on the assumption that the human body has two magnificent therapeutic centers: the immune system and what he calls "the pharmacy of the mind."

Researchers are finding a healthy brain can mix all kinds of medications in the right proportions and at the right times. Natural narcotics and other chemicals of the brain can go a long way toward alleviating discomfort, producing a sense of well-being, and healing one's body.

It's even possible for a vigorous immune system to overcome cancers, but unhealthy mental attitudes can severely restrict the healthy functioning of the brain. Resentments, fears, and hopelessness can actually block the immune system, according to Warner. Healing comes with the introduction of positive spiritual qualities: forgiveness, peace, hope, joy, and love.

Warner tells of a female University of Washington student diagnosed with terminal cancer. When they first met, she asked, "Can you keep me alive until I graduate?" She wanted to complete her education, which had been one of her goals. Warner couldn't supply any medical certainty, but he offered hope: "Do you want to graduate? Then we can make it!"

Upon her graduation, her request changed: "Can you keep me alive until my wedding?" She'd become engaged, and her marriage occupied center stage in her thoughts.

"You bet!" was the reply.

In a year or so, she was asking, "Can you keep me alive until I have a child?" The last I heard, she wanted to know if he could keep her alive until she became a grandmother! I wouldn't bet against it. Glen Warner gave her hope. He was more than a physician; he was a healer.

Lay people can't do brain surgery, but some of the key words used to explain illness are *stress, loneliness, resentment*. Healing comes when those negative emotions are replaced with love, purpose, and hope. The staff at the Menninger Foundation believes that if you get hope, you get well. Dr. Viktor Frankl connected healing to purpose. Norman Cousins wrote a book on the salubrious effects of joy. As Christians, we have all of those to offer in a ministry of healing and wholeness.

Finally, there is *prophetic ministry*, one that changes the way people live within the structures of society. Those practicing prophetic ministry look at the structures and ask, *How can they be changed for the better? How can I make a difference in medicine or law or education or business?*

Some concerned Christian lawyers in Seattle got together, saying, "The Bible says we shouldn't sue Christians. Let's find an alternative to our present court system." They came up with a plan to offer mediation and arbitration in disputes between Christians. For nearly a decade, the Christian Conciliation Service of Puget Sound has served the Seattle area. They hear cases for free or for a small fee, and they train people to solve disputes without resorting to costly and traumatic court proceedings.

Another man I know is working to find new ways to provide low-cost housing for the poor. He contends that churches don't have the money to underwrite housing on the scale that is needed, and Housing and Urban Development won't. His plan is to approach businesses and say, "Let me show you how you can build low-cost housing for the poor and make a reasonable profit." He's a prophet in the profit sector!

The Long Reach of the Laity

Another such prophet is a Rotary president and Mercedes-Benz/BMW dealer. I first met him at the Seattle Downtown Rotary, the second oldest and largest Rotary club in the world. We talked briefly about his volunteer work at an orthopedic hospital for children. It was, he said, the highlight of his life.

When he was elected president of the Downtown Rotary, he told me what he planned to do.

"Do you know what the motto of Rotary is?" he asked.

"Yes," I answered. "Service above self."

"Actually," he said, "most of us have spent our lives not having to give service. We've made money so we could hire secretaries and gatekeepers. We don't serve; we write checks. Well, I want to get Rotary practicing its beliefs. I want to get people in Rotary doing hands-on ministry in this city.

"There are many needy people: the hungry, the elderly, the homeless, the illiterate, the drug addicted, the unemployed. In July when I take office, I'm going to make every one of our eight hundred members choose an area to serve in for the next year. They can work in and with any organization they want. But they can't write a check; they've got to give service."

"Phil," I said, "are you prepared for the backlash you're going to get on this?"

His response moved me. "Bruce," he answered, "I heard you say one Sunday that people spend a lifetime accruing moral capital. I've done that. I've spent my life building up a good reputation selling cars with honesty and integrity, and doing volunteer work. I want to invest that moral capital before I die."

Phil did what he set out to do, and people are hearing about it. Other Rotary clubs are inviting him to speak about his plan, and the idea is spreading.

Those Rotarians have already helped many people in their volunteer work, but beyond that, they themselves will never be the same. Phil Smart began to change how those Rotarians viewed the city. I could never reach eight hundred people in Rotary, but Phil could and did.

The real measure of a church is the number of people in ministry, and central to pastoral care is putting people in ministry and supporting them in their ministries — material ministries, spiritual ministries, healing ministries, and prophetic ministries. That's getting back to basics. That's effective pastoral care.

True worship is directed first and foremost to the glory of God. But such worship, I've noticed, is also a means of pastoral care.

— Paul Anderson

Worship as Pastoral Care

One Saturday I met with a deeply distressed single parent. Since she had no church family, I encouraged her to worship with us on Sunday, which she did with her daughter. When the two of them came to see me on Monday, the daughter, obviously pleased with the release her mother experienced in worship, said, "Mom cried through the whole service."

Pastoral care of this woman began on Saturday and continued on Monday, but it wasn't complete without Sunday.

I like to think I listen sensitively and counsel wisely. I know, however, I often overestimate my part and underestimate God's part in pastoral care. When it comes to having concerns borne, people need a pastor, but they ultimately need to meet with the Almighty.

Like most congregations, we find people coming to us with deep and perplexing problems. We give them encouragement through personal counseling and support groups. But I also tell these people, "Worship with us. It will make a difference over the long haul." I've found that those who maintain regular worship heal faster.

True worship is directed first and foremost to the glory of God. But such worship, I've noticed, is also a means of pastoral care.

Worship Helps People Look Outside Themselves

I met for several weeks with a young man who didn't have serious psychological problems; he was just too focused on himself. He regularly turned conversations toward his concerns and would serve others only when it was convenient for him.

Over a few months, however, his attachment to self diminished. Now he pays more attention to others, showing more concern for their interests and needs. What made the difference?

"By praying daily and worshiping weekly," he said, "I became more aware of my self-centeredness."

Sometimes struggling people will find help only when they begin to look outside themselves toward heaven. Worship, because it focuses outward, can bring a healthy corrective to narcissism, as it did for my young friend. One cannot truly worship God and be fixated on one's self.

In an entertainment-oriented culture, however, it's sometimes difficult to keep the focus of worship on God. We're all tempted to think, at times, "I didn't get anything out of worship today," as if worship is primarily performed for our approval.

I enjoy the story of the man who complained to the minister following church, "I didn't like the hymns you chose today," to which the pastor replied, "That's okay; we weren't singing them for you."

Certainly, we must design services that are meaningful for worshipers. But if I want worship to help people pastorally, I must remind myself and my people that worshipers should first ask, "What does God think of my praise? What can I do for him?" The main test of worship is not how well the preacher has preached, but how well the worshipers have worshiped.

The paradox is that if we design worship to meet people's needs, we're less likely to help them, because we are leaving them in their self-oriented state. True worship, where giving to God is more important than getting, is the only worship that heals people of the tyranny of self.

Worship Dispels Loneliness

Struggles have a way of making us feel isolated. Worship, on the other hand, has a way of dispelling the feeling of isolation.

A woman who was coming off a bout with alcohol came to Christ and then started coming to our church, the first time on Good Friday. She told me she was very lonely. I told her, "Just keep coming, and it will make a difference." And although she struggled through her recovery, she's not lonely anymore. In fact, she has enough strength and self-confidence to reach out to other lonely people and invite them to church.

Worship can cure loneliness. It sets us in the midst of God's people, where the God who came "to save his people from their sins" (and not just me from my sin) promises to be with his people when they gather together. In worship it is no longer just "me and God" facing the world; it is "God and us."

For me liturgy is one means of driving home this reassuring truth. Confessing the ancient creeds together (especially that phrase from the Apostles' Creed: "I believe in the communion of saints . . .") reminds us that the church is bigger than we are and has been here longer than we have. Singing the *Kyrie* together ("Lord, have mercy") helps us identify with others who suffer. And the high point of our worship comes at the Eucharist, when we share together the life of Christ.

Forms that have a long tradition save us from assuming that the world centers around our needs. They put our troubles in perspective and help lonely people experience the healing that fellowship with Christian brothers and sisters, past and present, can bring.

For example, a single mother recently said she was unaccustomed to our Lutheran worship and somewhat intimidated by it at first. As she continued with us, however, she said she grew to appreciate our liturgy; it brought a needed security to her life. Her participation in worship invigorated the counseling we were providing.

Then again, a woman from a nonliturgical background who attended one Sunday told me afterward, "This place is dead." Her candid comment, whether accurate or not, highlights the danger of liturgy. While tradition can breed security, it may appear to be the security of sleep.

There's the old joke about a Pentecostal man who once wandered into a liturgical worship service. As the pastor preached, the man responded with, "Praise the Lord!"

A woman finally turned around and scolded him, "Excuse me, but we don't praise the Lord in the Lutheran church."

But a man down the pew corrected her, "Yes we do; it's on page 19."

Although liturgy can help, we know it isn't the sole answer. So we try regularly to bridge the past and present, form and freedom. For example, we include free times of prayer as a part of corporate liturgical responses. We also sing the great hymns of the church along with the more contemporary worship songs.

In short, worship that is grounded in tradition and responsive to the Spirit can remind people, especially lonely people who feel isolated in their troubles, that there is a community larger than themselves with whom they can pray and be comforted.

Worship Helps People Step Out in Hope

Ralph Martin writes in *The Worship of God* that the act of praise is a "dialogue, involving the interchange of the divine initiative and the human response. Worship pulsates with a two-beat rhythm expressed simply as 'we come to God' and 'God comes to us.' "

When we recognize that worship is divine initiation *and* human response, it can become a means of unlocking people from personal moods.

When people face enormous problems, it's easy for them to get discouraged, which leads to passivity, which, in turn, can lead to more discouragement. People become chained in a tight circle of hopelessness. Worship breaks into that circle by requiring people to do something — something positive and hopeful — to give glory to God.

King David didn't always feel upbeat. Yet even in his discouraged moments, he could pray, "I will bless the Lord at all times. His praise shall continually be in my mouth" (Ps. 34:1). I believe that kept him from despondent inactivity.

Our custodian, John, became a Christian out of a life of drugs and crime. When we hired him, he was still struggling to break free from his past. Singing was one thing that helped stabilize John. In fact, we always knew where John was working because he sang all day. As he sang the songs and hymns he learned in worship, the Holy Spirit reprogrammed his mind, replacing darkness with light.

Praise enlists worshipers in active response to God — "with hearts and hands and voices." After acting in hope, people become more hopeful.

Fine-Tuning Worship for Pastoral Care

Since we recognize these effects of worship on people, here are some ways we shape our services.

To highlight the fact that no one stands alone, I hug everyone I can on Sunday. Many don't get that even from their nuclear family. A hug tells people they're special, even those who make me feel like I'm embracing a telephone pole.

We also give care to specific individuals in the service. Before one Mother's Day service, Lynn was feeling down and had requested prayer. Before coming to faith in Christ, she had left her teenage children, and although she had received a new family since, she hadn't yet reconciled with her past.

During the service, I shared her concern (with her permission) with the congregation, and then I asked some people near her to gather around her as I prayed. "I felt loved," Lynn said afterward, as she thanked me.

Seeing worship as pastoral care has raised my expectations for the service and changed the way I approach it. Since God can save people from all sorts of trouble, I am more careful to share the gospel as a part of each sermon.

Since God will release people from the power of sin, I lead the liturgical confession of sins and absolution with the sense that spiritual life depends on them. We pray for people by name during the service, whether the request is healing for body, soul, or spirit.

Preparing for worship, then, means more than preparing a sermon. In fact, when I find myself spending ten hours on a sermon and fifteen minutes throwing together a worship service, I'm not properly acknowledging the importance of the pastoral care dynamic of worship.

Helping People Meet the "Wonderful Counselor"

People need God more than they need me. It is God who can ultimately encourage, change, heal, and comfort them. Worship is a primary means of helping people see God in the midst of their troubled lives. Counseling and the Sunday service, then, have the same goal in mind: to put people in touch with the healing power of God.

After one service, a woman said to me, "I don't know why, but I started crying as soon as we started singing." I have heard that often from new people. It is not the brilliance of singers or the professionalism of instrumentalists; it is the sense of God's presence that moves them.

One Sunday we invited someone I thought was a guest

preacher. He didn't preach, however; he sat down at the piano and led us in worship. In a gentle and joyful way, he brought us into the presence of God.

My secretary later commented about that service, "During the worship time, the Holy Spirit was teaching me many things — things I needed to do, things I needed to say, areas I needed to give up to the Lord.

"When our guest stopped playing, I thought he was going to start preaching. What I hadn't realized is that he had taken the entire time for worship and that he didn't intend to preach. At first I felt let down, but then I realized how much the Lord had helped me just through the worship."

In sum, Jesus, the "Wonderful Counselor," knows better than I how to get through to people. He sends the Paraclete, the Helper, to come alongside people. So although I don't schedule counseling appointments on Sunday, God often does — right during the worship service.

On people's jobs, in the local grocery and hardware stores, at the post office and service station, and on the town's sidewalks, the pastor can build strong relationships and perform vital ministry, ministry that cannot happen in any other way.

— Doug Self

CHAPTER FOUR

Ministering in the Marketplace

Larry died a few years ago in a work-related accident. His office building exploded, and Larry didn't make it. Although Larry is gone, as well as the office where we'd spent a lot of time together, I cherish the relationship we had and thank God for it.

Because he was connected with our church, I visited him regularly, usually at his work. The receptionist would take my name and buzz him on the intercom. Sometimes it might take a few minutes for him to get loose, but he always had a big smile as he rounded the corner and stuck out his hand. Then we'd walk back to his office for a brief chat. He'd often introduce me to others in the hallways or in their offices. Larry and I would sit in his office for a few minutes, sometimes for half an hour if he didn't have urgent business. We'd talk about his job, his family, whatever was of interest to him.

A few times he ran into difficulties on his job. On those occasions we'd meet somewhere for lunch, and he'd give me the details of the problem. Because I had an understanding of his work, he trusted me to give him biblical counsel about those situations.

That experience has reinforced for me the value of pastoral care in the marketplace. On people's jobs, in the local grocery and hardware stores, at the post office and service station, and on the town's sidewalks, the pastor can build strong relationships and perform vital ministry, ministry that cannot happen in any other way.

In many ways, pastoral care in the marketplace is more challenging than in the church or hospital, where the rules are more clear. Although I'm continually learning, here are some insights I've gained over the years that help me do it better.

Be a Person as Well as a Parson

Confusing one's personal identity with one's professional role is a danger, especially for a pastor. Sometimes we play the pastoral role too thoroughly.

If people in other professions did this, we'd laugh. I sometimes imagine the fire chief shopping at the local grocery store. He wears his heavy fireman's coat and hat with visor. As he pushes his cart around, he encounters the local populace, saying, "Hello, John. Keeping that chimney clean?" or, "Hey, Gladys, I thought I saw your children playing with matches the other day. Let's keep a closer watch on them, okay?" and to the new resident, "Hello, I'm Fireman Bill. Do you have any flammables stored in your garage?"

He'd be a one-dimensional guy with a fireman veneer, always conscious of being the fire chief and directing all his relationships accordingly. People soon would tire of him and say, "Hey, Bill, what's with this fireman bit? Can't we talk about the Broncos or fishing sometimes?"

As pastors, we live in the world of theological issues, commentaries, church life, and the like. It can be hard to change gears in casual conversation. Our comments and questions might never stray from the ecclesiastical: "Mrs. Smith, glad I ran into you. How's the kitchen committee?" or "Hi, George. What did you think of last Sunday's service?"

There's nothing wrong with talking about such issues. But especially in the marketplace, we're wise to engage in other topics. I don't want people to relate only to an image of a minister, but to me, a person God called to ministry. Only when I engage people in genuine conversation, minus my stained-glass voice and pastoral-care tone, can I adequately perform marketplace ministry.

Put People at Ease

Even when we avoid playing the pastoral role, sometimes people will try to put us in it anyway. They feel they need to clean up their language, stand straight, and talk about religious things to the minister. Not much ministry can take place if this barrier stands in the way of genuine conversation.

This is a particular problem when people become guilty in our presence because they've missed a committee meeting or several weeks of worship. Sometimes people ought to feel guilty for such, but there's no need to play on it. I find I can better care for them if I can put them at ease.

For example, I spotted Fred and Phyllis in the vegetable section of the grocery store. Fred began looking nervous when he saw me. We both knew he'd spent last Sunday at the lake with their new boat. When Phyllis looked around and saw me, she became visibly uncomfortable, as well.

I walked toward them, pushing my cart and smiling. Fred spoke first, "Hello, Pastor. Uh, sorry we missed church last week. You know we've got that new boat and uh — "

"Hey, Fred, Phyllis! How are you doing?" I interjected.

"Fine," they muttered.

"I saw a boat in your driveway last week. What a beauty! What kind of engine has it got?"

Fred, although a little off balance, warmed to his favorite subject: "Oh, that. Well, we went ahead and got the super engine instead of the standard. That'll let us pull all three of the kids on skis at one time."

"I bet it really moves. How fast does it go without skiers behind?"

Fred's eyes lit up. "Well, Phyllis doesn't like for me to run it so fast, but once, on Sunday afternoon, after I let Phyllis and the girls off at the dock, Randy and I opened her up. We were doing maybe fifty-five, but the lake began to get a little choppy. It'll probably do a little more."

By then they were looking at me like the Cratchets eyed Scrooge when he showed up with the turkey.

"I'd sure like to go with you sometime," I continued. "I used to do some water-skiing. Used to be able to get up on one ski, in fact. I'd like to ski behind a boat like that."

"Well, Randy and I are going out again Saturday morning. We'd love to have you go with us."

I don't have to go skiing with everyone who has a boat. But I can try to put people at ease when they are uncomfortable in my presence.

Maybe Fred and Phyllis should have been in church. Maybe they should have increased their giving to the church instead of buying the boat. And maybe they would seldom attend church that summer. But they're going to boat and ski anyway. I can plague them about it every time I see them, or I can accept their decision.

When I can appreciate their enjoyment of their new boat and time with their family, I may be able even to use the boat to build a better relationship with them. Then I'll still be able to pastor them throughout the summer as I have the chance. And they'll be more apt to return to regular church attendance in the fall.

Know Something about Subjects of Local Interest

I've had pastors tell me they have no patience with small talk. They claim that unless they're conversing about spiritual matters, they feel restless. They think small talk is a waste of time.

Yet small talk makes a big impression. People size us up in these casual encounters. They want to know if we're familiar with the world they live in. Being able to talk Little League baseball, high school sports, community government, gas prices, and the weather all signal that the pastor is in touch with their world. Then they listen to sermons with more confidence.

I invested many hours in emergency medical training so I could serve on the local rescue squad. Learning about triage, bandaging, and splinting gave me a conversational entrée with many people of our community. Describing some of the drama of the squad's work made for powerful sermon illustrations. And besides helping people in medical emergencies, I also made lasting friendships with fellow squad members.

Listen to Others as If You Respect Them

Naturally, it would be best to listen to others *because* I respect them. But I admit sometimes I'm not there yet. At those times, I recognize I have to start somewhere.

Once in a while at a denominational meeting, I meet a peer or superior I wish I hadn't. The other clergy person appears glad to see me, but the conversation is soon dominated by his accomplishments. I can't open up about my own struggles and (gulp) failures, at least not while Captain Success is unfurling the banner of personal achievements. Even if I do speak, I feel I wouldn't be respected by this expert in church work.

Then again, I've talked often with a ministerial friend who genuinely cares about me and respects me. When that happens, I feel like I'm in an oasis. Someone understands the difficulties I face; eyes remain on me, and body language says, "I'm listening. What you're saying is important. What you're doing in ministry is important."

So when I talk with people, I try to see their experiences from their point of view. I try to listen with genuine interest to another's ideas, even if the notions are flawed; at this point, they are the best the person has.

Craig struck me as a shallow, plastic Christian. Rather than seeking Christ's direction for himself, he merely imitated the social behavior of Christian leaders around him. Instead of dealing with doubts and questions so he could go deeper, he merely swept them under the rug.

In working with him, however, I felt it was important to begin by discovering his perspective on his faith, to understand why he avoided a deeper walk. I tried to discover how he discovered his spiritual beliefs. I wanted to know and respect the place from which he started. Only when I was sure that I comprehended his position did I dare suggest he go further.

Even if I don't have an opportunity in a conversation to suggest further growth, listening carefully to the other person is still worthwhile. I may have given that person a treasure, the feeling that he or she is important to the pastor, that his or her religious experiences are worthy of pastoral consideration.

Keep Looking Beneath Casual Conversations

Listening with respect means more than keeping quiet while the other talks. Over the years, as I've learned to evaluate "casual" comments, I've learned how to be a better pastor.

When I talk with a church member in the store or post office, although the conversation may be brief, he or she may touch on a variety of subjects:

- the weather: "It's hotter than usual."

- children: "Billy's a little uneasy with his first year in junior high."

- career: "My wife is expecting a promotion and a raise."

- home: "We're winding up summer home-improvement projects, painting trim and replacing awnings."

- community: "I'm opposed to the new zoning they're proposing for our neighborhood."

- family: "We weren't able to get away on a vacation this summer."

- personal matters: "I'd promised myself that I would lose those extra pounds this summer, but obviously I've failed again."

- church: "I've been on the building and grounds committee for three years now. I think it's time I stepped aside."

As we talk, I evaluate each part of the conversation as negative, neutral, or positive, and make a mental note about how I might respond. For example, in the above conversation:

- the weather — neutral.

- children — somewhat negative. Ask Billy about his school experience at the next opportunity.

- career — positive. Congratulate his wife on her accomplishment at the next opportunity.

- home — positive. Reinforce their enjoyment of accomplishment and working together.

- community — negative. Ask for his opinion and become more knowledgeable about the issue.

- family — negative. Ask where they'd planned to go. Who's most disappointed? What stresses and pressures did they most need a vacation from?

- personal matters — negative. Ask about any health problems with the current weight.

- church — negative. Ask what she has been able to accomplish during her tenure. Find out the difficulties of the job. What were the personal rewards of the task?

Of these eight subjects, several may warrant follow-up. Consider the following:

- family — negative. From my preliminary questions, I may discover several stresses in this family. This can help me as I plan sermons and church programming for families. I may want to drop by their home for an extended visit to bring these issues to the surface.

- personal — negative. Ask how she feels about the inability to lose weight. Ask about her self-perception at her present size. A counseling appointment might be appropriate to work on healthy self-esteem. Many overweight people loathe themselves.

● church — negative. I might discover a person who has served without adequate recognition and appreciation, or a person who has been trying to do a job without adequate resources. I could use this opportunity to encourage and thank the person and become more sensitive to those who serve the church behind the scenes.

So, seemingly casual conversations contain a wealth of pastoral-care potential. People bring up subjects, feelings, needs, and interests that the alert pastor can use to discover issues that need pastoral attention.

See People on the Job

Since people attend church only a few hours a week, I try to invest some of my time with people where they spend much of their time: at work.

In the early years of my ministry, I'd visit farms in the community where I served. It was fairly easy to spend a few minutes with agricultural folk. I'd wait at the end of the turn-row. When the farmer pulled up in the tractor, he'd shut it down for a few minutes' conversation.

Or I might work with the person I'd visit. I might drive the tractor, or brand calves, or whatever. I understood their work better, and they got to see how I operated on their turf, and the latter often prompted good-natured laughter.

There aren't many farmers or ranchers in my congregation now, nor do many pastors minister in agricultural settings. Most people work in shops and office buildings spread over a city. They're harder to see on the job. But that only increases the value of a pastor's visit.

Naturally, I try to be sensitive to the work situation. Sometimes company policy forbids nonemployees on the job. In other cases, I can visit only with permission. Some employees I have to meet before or after work. Although most supervisors appreciate help from others who are concerned about the well-being of employees, it's always wise to check with them ahead of time. So before I visit, I ask the person for the name of his supervisor so I can explain to him what I'm about.

But in spite of these few obstacles, I find visiting on the job has a number of benefits.

● *It shows a pastor cares.* A number of the men in our church are in the construction trade. One man works as a painter, another as a wallpaper hanger. Some are finish carpenters. Others are framers. They work in several communities in all stages of construction.

I find out where they're working and try to drop by once or twice while they're on that job. On large home and commercial construction, it can be quite a treasure hunt to find them, but when I do, their faces always light up. By visiting them at their place of work, around which a great deal of their lives revolves, I communicate, "Your pastor cares about you and your life."

● *People's daily work is valued.* Soon after one women in our congregation had begun working for a property-management company, I drove an hour to see her on the job. She recently had divorced and was forced to find work to support herself and her small children.

I entered through a glass door and met the receptionist. As she greeted me, Carolyn, who had been talking to co-workers close by, visibly brightened and asked, "Doug, what are you doing here?"

"Well, I came to see you," I answered. "You look like a high-powered executive. Where's your office?"

Obviously pleased, she led me past her wondering co-workers to her cubicle. Since she'd just joined the company, it was a small work space, but hers. She sat behind her desk, and I sat in the chair in front of it.

"You mean you came all this way to see me?" she asked.

I explained that several other church members worked in the same town and that I'd come to see them, as well, but added, "I especially wanted to see you on your new job and pray for you, if that would be possible."

She was delighted and said she felt honored that I'd come to see her. We chatted a few minutes about her work. I sensed this shouldn't be a long visit in her busy office, so I looked around to make sure we had some privacy, and, looking at her, prayed, "Almighty God, we thank you for the opportunity to work hard, make money, and accomplish things. I pray for Carolyn in her work here that you would bless her with wisdom and efficiency. In Christ's name we pray. Amen." She smiled and stood to see me to the door.

Not only could I affirm her in her new job, I was able to pray with her and "bless" her daily endeavors, reminding her of Christ's presence in that place.

● *Opportunities develop for deeper ministry.* One of our church's men was a truck driver. Every day he drove a load of heavy freight to a mine in the next valley. After I got to know him, he invited me to ride with him on one of his runs.

He left early — 4:30 A.M. — so I arrived at the maintenance garage a little after four with my Thermos of coffee, as he'd advised. I met his fellow workers, he loaded his truck, and off we went. We spent several hours together as we made our way to the mine. I learned a lot about him and his job.

Another man in our church sells industrial products. When his sales calls will be brief and low-key, he invites me to join him. We talk as he drives between calls.

One day while I was riding with him on his rounds, he was obviously hesitant. He wanted to talk about something, but didn't know exactly whether or how to bring it up. But because we were spending extended time together, he finally was able to get it out. It was a deep concern he felt was inhibiting his Christian life and witness. He and some of the other men at church had talked about it but didn't know what to do. On this trip, we were able to discuss it.

● *Christ's teaching can be brought to bear on the job.* Greg worked in a local manufacturing operation, a small shop with less than ten employees. After he and his family began attending church, I visited him briefly on the job. Before long, he began to complain about conflicts and pressures at work. He especially complained about "the stupidity and insensitivity" of his boss, who had been denying him pay raises and assigning Greg to less glamorous jobs.

When Greg began describing this as an attack of Satan through a non-Christian boss, I asked if it would help if I talked with his boss. He said it might.

I had met the employer, and he seemed friendly enough. So I made an appointment with him at the end of the day, after the employees had gone home. Knowing I was this employee's pastor, he was genuinely curious about our visit.

After assuring him I wanted Greg to be a productive and harmonious worker, I said, "It appears that Greg is having some difficulty at work. He's indicated that he's being passed up for promotion and assigned entry-level tasks. That tells me there are some things about Greg you're not pleased with."

The boss nodded agreement but still appeared curious.

I continued, "As Greg's pastor, I'm concerned about his character development. You must feel Greg isn't being as productive as he should or that he's being disruptive. You have a bottom-line financial equation you have to balance, and Greg must not be contributing toward that end. I'd like to know what deficiencies or problems you see in Greg so that I could work with him as his pastor. I won't tell Greg specifically what you tell me, but I will work with him on weaknesses you point out."

Greg's employer didn't know exactly how to respond. It sounded like he had the equivalent of an industrial psychologist offering to help him with a problem employee. He soon warmed to the idea. He had no problem talking about Greg's problems and was able to illustrate his concerns with specific examples. I listened carefully and took notes, and together we honed in on the character traits Greg would need to work on.

Greg's boss then asked me how he could deal more effectively with Greg. He recognized Greg could be a valuable employee but was hindered by these issues. Since I knew Greg had been raised by a demanding, never-pleased father, I suggested the boss balance necessary criticism with praise.

Greg and I spent several sessions together in which we discussed these traits in light of biblical principles. Approached in a different manner and by someone other than his boss, Greg responded positively and set about to make some changes. Those changes took awhile, but Greg and his boss are now getting along much better.

Some might think that's a lot of time and effort to invest in one person. But for me, that's what pastoring is about. Discipleship means helping individuals apply Christian principles in daily life — what Greg and I did. As a result, I've developed a deeper relationship with Greg and a credible relationship with Greg's non-Christian boss. In addition, Greg is more effective in his ministry in our church because he's not so troubled by his job.

● *Ministry is performed for the community.* Several years ago the miners at a local coal mine went on strike. They picketed the mine entrance and soon nonunion workers began crossing the picket line. Tempers flared, and some ugly confrontations ensued.

I began going to the picket line with another elder, early in the mornings during shift change. Around a roaring fire stood a knot of miners. We'd visit with them for a while and pick up the latest developments and rumors. Then we'd go over by a large rock, kneel, and pray for the miners, the "scabs," and the management. We prayed for peace and for a mutually advantageous settlement. The miners appreciated our presence, and some new relationships were formed.

Granted, this is an unusual situation. But such unusual opportunities for ministry to the community occur more often when I try to carry pastoral care into the workplace.

There's no formula for successful marketplace ministry. In fact, sometimes it's threatening to venture out. I'm more at home in a church setting, where I know what's expected of me. But I continue to go outside the church walls and look for ways I can care for people pastorally in the department store, on the job, on the sidewalk.

For me, meeting people on their turf is what the Incarnation was about.

PART TWO

Special Concerns

A church is not a clinic in which a faceless and interchangeable staff services the clientele by showing up and handing out pills. The staff of a church is a living, breathing family. We may wrestle at times. We may injure one another sometimes and rescue each other at others. But we're in it together and need one another.

— *Bruce Larson*

CHAPTER FIVE
Caring for Key Leaders

For several years in Seattle, I owned a sailboat that I loved to take out on Puget Sound to get away from it all. I kept a picture of it on my desk, and it provided a fantasy outlet for me. *If things get really bad*, I thought, *I can get on that boat and sail right out of here!*

Well, things never got that bad, thanks to the fact that so many people were caring for me, not the least of those being my wife, Hazel (in spite of the fact that last year she talked me into selling the boat!). Actually, Hazel and I have understood our need for care since my first pastorate.

That first church out of Princeton Seminary was in Binghamton, New York, where I was associate pastor. Hazel and I had been married during my last year of seminary, and ten months later our first baby arrived. Then four months after that, a second baby was on the way. All the changes in our lives took a toll. Mad and frantic, and with our marriage in serious trouble, we reached out in desperation to two lay couples in the church who were also new parents. "We're going through a terrible time," we confessed.

They surprised us by saying, "So are we!"

So we decided to meet with them to pray and read the Bible. Those meetings turned us around and saved three marriages. But beyond that, genuine new life broke out, and within a year, a number of groups were meeting. By the next year, there must have been a hundred such groups gathering out of that little church in downtown Binghamton. People were drawn to the kind of intimacy and caring we distressed couples had stumbled upon.

We went from Binghamton to Boston, where I studied psychology at Boston University. After earning a master's degree, I was called to pastor a church in Pana, a small town in the lush corn and soybean fields of central Illinois. I tried to impose on those dear folks what I had learned. Not knowing that the conspiracy against intimacy can be enormous in a small town, I experienced little success, and I began to feel lonely and disheartened.

I'll never forget lying in bed in our tiny, unair-conditioned bedroom late one sweltering summer night. A Rock Island train was crossing the sultry prairie, and we could hear its distant whistle. Hazel turned to me and sighed, "I wish I were on that train going anyplace."

"Me, too," I replied in frustration. "Me, too."

By the time we left a few years later, we did have a couple of groups functioning, and many lives were changed by Jesus Christ. I am grateful for our years in Pana, for they taught me that intimate support groups — and especially getting church leaders into such groups — won't always be a popular thing.

Later, after twenty-one years in parachurch ministry, I was offered the pastorate of University Presbyterian Church (UPC) in

Seattle. At least one friend, who knew the size and scope of the ministry there, advised, "Don't go. It will kill you." But I went anyway.

Once I was there, however, I discovered that my four predecessors had left under unhappy circumstances. I panicked and called out for help at an elders' retreat. "They tell me this church can be pretty hard on senior pastors," I said, "but I hope to leave here someday in my right mind and still praising the Lord. To do that, I need your help. Who would like to volunteer to meet with me once a week for ninety minutes on Friday mornings?"

Six men came up to me during the retreat and offered to join me. For ten years we "Seven Dwarfs" met quietly out of the flow of church traffic to talk about our lives, our families, our Lord, our finances — anything but church shop talk. To put it another way, they were my pastors during those years.

Through my years in ministry, I've recognized my need for continuing care as a pastor. And if *I* need it, so do the other leaders — the staff and elders. Ministry is too tough to go it alone. Lay leaders and staff need pastoral care as much, if not more, than men and women in pews.

A Model for Models

In churches as large as University Presbyterian or the Crystal Cathedral, obviously I cannot be available to every person who walks in off the street. But I've had a policy that members can always see me. If it's not urgent, it may take a couple of weeks to get an appointment, but I am available. I need to be, if, for nothing else, to be a relevant preacher, one who is aware of the hurts and needs of the congregation.

But for me, pastoral care centers on the staff and elders, or church officers. They're the ones I pastor first; they get the major part of my time and attention. For example, at UPC we had thirty-six elders on Session and twelve program staff members. Those forty-eight people were my primary responsibility.

Modeling, we're told, is the most effective teaching method. Early on, I learned that if I want a tithing church, I have to tithe. If I want a praying church, I must pray. And if I want a small-group church, I need to be in a small group.

So in my ministry, I strive to model how an authentic leader relates to other people. As the elders and staff observe my ministry style, my priorities, my way of approaching life, I hope they will see certain qualities: openness, vulnerability, the ability to put people ahead of assignments, a steadfast commitment to the Lord, and a genuine relationship with him.

If the staff and elders take up this style of ministry, then they, in turn, become models for the church. People are watching them and observing their lifestyle to discern what this Christian life is all about. That's why I tell our elders, "Your primary job is not to draw up budgets, spend the money, and run committees. Rather, it is to demonstrate how the family of God behaves. We need to be upfront if we're angry (instead of carrying resentment), preferring one another in love, quick to support and help one another. The people of the church are watching us closely. They see the quality of our relationships with the Lord and with one another."

One phrase seems to sum up that philosophy for our Session: Elders are not simply big-E elders, who serve Communion, spend money, and decide programs; we are also small-e elders, who are ministers who care for people, beginning with the other elders. This kind of mutual caregiving between the church staff and elders is bound to permeate the entire congregation.

Caring for Staff

What are my pastoral-care concerns for staff members? I want to encourage them to be real people, not super saints. My first concern isn't that they produce tremendous amounts of work (which, of course, I wouldn't discourage), but that I help leaders realize they can cry, they can say no when there is too much on their plate, they can take a day off without guilt. Mainly I want them to remain genuine and spiritually healthy.

For instance, one pastor leading worship began the prayer of confession: "Lord, I'm sorry I put my fist through the wall this week." We could all picture that much better than vague generalities about falling short of God's best and not doing some things we ought to have done. There is no power in confessing we are generic sinners. But when we say something like, "Lord, I was preoccupied with selling my house this week and neglected you," that's specific confession. That helps people grow in their understanding of godliness. And that's the kind of staff member I want my pastoral care to enable and encourage.

Staff members have a great deal of responsibility in any congregation, so the weekly staff meeting is an important time that ought to include more than job-related problems. Staff members need personal support as well.

One former associate just came through a divorce. His wife left him and their four children after twenty years of marriage. He continued on staff through this trauma, and the church wept with him and grew with him. It was tough for him to be a homemaker and father and pastor. But at his time of heartbreak, he had a pastor and a church to share his hurt and share his ministry.

This kind of pastoral relationship within a staff doesn't come automatically because offices line the same hall; it has to be developed — usually by the head of staff. When Hazel and I arrived at UPC in 1980, we invited the four other pastors and their wives to our home for dinner. I made my two-alarm chili, and we talked and dreamed the evening away. When they left, Hazel said, "Didn't that feel good! Let's do it again."

"We can't make a practice of this," I protested. "I may have to fire someone, and I can't do it if we're the best of friends."

"Oh, let's just try it," Hazel urged, not willing to let me off the hook. So twice a month we met at our home for dessert and sometimes dinner. We met as a family. We laughed and cried and weathered tough times in some of our lives. What we did was blur the image between the professional and the personal. I know that may fly in the face of some management advice, but it worked for us. I sometimes had to lay down the law as head of staff, but when I did, I had the advantage of knowing the staff members, and they, in turn, knew and understood me. We became intimate friends, family even. Sure, we were competitive and insecure sometimes, but we were family, so when one scored a goal, everyone cheered.

I sometimes consider how different this is from a lot of church staffs. One senior pastor I know hasn't spoken to one of his staff members for five years. I can't believe this kind of strain doesn't show up on Sunday mornings when both stand before the congregation to lead worship.

A church is not a clinic, in which a faceless and interchangeable staff services the clientele by showing up and handing out pills. I believe the staff of a church is a living, breathing family. We may wrestle at times. We may injure one another sometimes and rescue each other at others. But we're in it together and need one another. Ministry is not my profession; it's my *life*. My colleagues are not mere co-workers; they're my brothers and sisters.

Caring for Lay Leaders

My plan for pastoral care of the leaders begins with an emphasis on the three essentials of the Christian faith.

1. *An encounter with the living Lord.* Basic to Christian life is an experience of God's power and presence. Many churches are full of unconverted believers who assent to right theology, down to the last "I believe" in the Apostles' Creed, but who nevertheless wonder deep down, *What good does it do me?* They've given their money and their time to the church, but they've never met Christ Jesus.

As a pastor, I need to begin by ensuring that each elder has actually had an encounter with the living Lord. Some elders with forty years of service in the church have just begun to learn to talk with Christ and listen to him and know his presence.

One elder tells a memorable story of how he became a Christian. He heard an evangelistic team speak about the new life, and, as the meeting ended, Pete said to a team member, "I can't give my life to Jesus with integrity. I have commitments for the next three years."

So the evangelist asked, "Well, how about next week? Is that free?"

"No, it's not," he replied. "I'm already committed."

"Then how about the next twenty-four hours? Would you

turn your life over to Christ for the next twenty-four hours?"

"Well, I guess I can do that," Pete replied, and he did. He never took it back.

2. *The experience of koinonia.* I'm convinced people want and need to know others on a deep and personal level and be known by them, but they're terrified of rejection. They've been rejected so many times they're afraid of reaching out again. They are determined to avoid anything personal. They'll do Bible studies, take on projects, bring in speakers, and discuss Christian books — anything but talk about their lives, their failings, their needs.

Yet, however much some tend to avoid it, church leaders need to be a part of the body; they need to experience *koinonia.* Jesus' commandment was, after all, to "love one another as I have loved you." Intimacy is scary, but Jesus first modeled it for church leaders when he gathered the Twelve.

My need for *koinonia* led to those weekly meetings with the Seven Dwarfs. And to meet that same need for all the leaders, we divided the Session at UPC into "families" of six or seven who gathered at the beginning of Session meetings to catch up on one another and share joys and burdens. The members of these families soon began to take on the pastoral care of one another.

I remember a typical Session meeting with an enormous docket, which ordinarily would have kept the Session until after midnight. With the Session families meeting first, however, we were finished with the entire meeting by 9:40. Why?

There's an obvious reason. People come to such meetings with baggage — a rocky marriage, a job in jeopardy, health problems. They may arrive angry or guilty or anxious. But meeting first with six other caring friends, they can work on those issues; then personal matters don't become enmeshed with the business portion of the meeting. Elders don't veto somebody's initiative in the business meeting because they're mad at the world.

Session retreats are another way to build *koinonia.* Several years ago we used the Book of Galatians as the basis for our retreat. In that letter, Paul tells his story in the first two chapters, declares his beliefs in the second two, and shares his ministry in the last two.

I suggested we divide our retreat into thirds and cover those same three topics. On the first night three elders told their stories, and the next day, all the elders told their life stories in their Session families. By telling and hearing such touching, intimate histories, that Session experienced *koinonia*.

Koinonia promotes accountability. Pastors and elders can sometimes get out of line, but when structures like our Session families are in place, there's someone to say, "Hey! Just what do you think you're doing?" In this setting, people care about us — enough to keep us from error. Even better, the pastor doesn't have to do all the "straightening out." Each staff member and elder has a Session family to hold him or her accountable.

For instance, when one man from my small group suddenly walked out on his wife of twenty-seven years, I talked with him. But mine was only one of nearly a dozen contacts from fellow group members. All lovingly listened to him, prayed with him, and asked him pointedly, "Can this really be what God wants?" He had a whole lot of "pastors" caring for him.

3. *The exercise of ministry.* Most church leaders have some ministry within the church. They may head up the Sunday school or coordinate the ushers or lead Bible studies. These activities are almost a given. But the ministry I encourage these people to do takes place outside the church walls.

I make a point of visiting each of my elders in their workplace. When I first began doing this, they suspected I came to solicit their help for the church. After touring the workplace and greeting colleagues, we'd go out to eat, and my lunch partner was invariably wondering, *Okay, when's he going to ask me to do something?*

They were surprised to find I was not there to recruit them. "I just want to know how your ministry is going at work. How do you see your ministry here at Boeing? (or Nordstrom? or Swedish Hospital?)" When conversation turned to Session assignments, I'd underscore that I was there to talk about the ministry at work and at home with the family.

Ministry takes many forms, but there is nothing more rewarding than being the one by whom lonely, desperate, drowning people find new life and purpose in the person of Jesus Christ.

A chemist friend tells this unique story. A man at the laboratory approached him one day with a confession. "Earl, I envy you. My life is a mess, but obviously something is different about you. I figure it has something to do with Jesus, because I've heard you talking about him. But I have a problem with Jesus." These two Ph.D.'s discussed the Christian faith at length without a breakthrough. Finally, Earl turned to his friend and asked, "Can you make a turnip?"

"Of course not," the fellow replied, a little surprised. "No chemist can make a turnip."

"Then would you be willing to turn your life over to the Great Turnip Maker?" Earl pressed.

The fellow chemist thought a minute and replied, "Yeah, I could to that," and they prayed together. It wasn't long before Earl's friend discovered that the Great Turnip Maker was none other than Jesus Christ himself. He read in John's gospel, chapter 1, "All things are made by him, and without him was not anything made that was made." And Earl had the joy of seeing his friend find what proved to be genuine faith.

Ministry takes place all week long in all we do at the workplace, yes, but also in our homes and in our neighborhoods. A developer and his wife, both in their late 30s, moved into a massive new home in an area he was developing. It was a neighborhood with enormous homes surrounded by big lots, so it wasn't easy to get to know neighbors. Unhappy with that situation, these two opened their home at Advent for a beautiful, candlelight dinner for about a hundred neighbors. The fellowship was so warm and genuine that they decided to keep the meetings going. Now they have regular gatherings there, and in addition to dinner, they invite a guest speaker to share his or her witness. This young couple ministers to the whole development.

Church leaders can be viewed in two ways: as workers to fill leadership slots or as fellow ministers who need special pastoral care commensurate with their added responsibilities. I, of course, choose the latter.

But this pastoral care is not the job only of the senior pastor. Church leaders, lay and clergy, can learn to pastor each other. After all, we need one another, not just to perform ministry, but to be the body of Christ: mothers, fathers, sisters, and brothers to each other.

Inactives are people who hurt. They need more than a scolding to become active in church. They also need pastoral care.

— Doug Self

CHAPTER SIX

Strategies for Ministering to Inactives

D*ropouts, delinquents, do-nothings, lazy, backsliders, complainers,* and *excuse makers.* These are words regular church attenders often use to describe inactives. In *Ministry to Inactives* (Augsburg, 1979), Gerhard Knutson documents these attitudes. He tells of one study that revealed that regular church attenders tend to use the following words to describe their feelings about inactives: *frustrated, fearful, anxious, worried, hostile, suspicious, sympathetic, puzzled,* and *embarrassed.*

In my experience, active members aren't hostile to inactives, but they are puzzled as to why they no longer attend. Especially after unsuccessfully reaching out to inactives, active members can become frustrated and, inadvertently, begin badmouthing them.

It's no wonder, then, that inactives, as revealed in the same study, describe active church people as *hypocrites, do-gooders, nosy, fussy, nit-pickers, bosses, "in group," judges, high and mighty,* and *meddlers.* And inactives describe themselves in relation to the church as *condemned, forgotten, left out, lonely, rejected, abandoned, angry, suspicious,* and *apathetic.*

Inactives, then, are people who hurt. They need more than a scolding to become active in church. They also need pastoral care.

And since inactives probably view me, the pastor, as the embodiment of the church, I need to be especially sensitive to their feelings about the church.

Pastoral care to inactives, like all pastoral care, must be approached case by case. I've found, in fact, that I need to employ a variety of strategies if I am going to minister to them effectively. Here are some of the most common.

Listen to Expert Testimony

Glen would attend church with his family for several months, then miss a month, and then come once and miss two more months. Then he'd repeat the whole cycle again.

Early on I had Glen pegged: he was unfaithful. He seemed to let slight colds and camping preempt his church attendance. More than once I went to Glen's door with a reprimand ready.

We would visit casually at first, and then I would bring up his absences. He would wince, and, as I was about to launch into a gentle diatribe, he would confide in me about problems he was having with his children from a previous marriage. His oldest daughter, for example, was rebellious and trying drugs.

Over time I discovered that some weekends Glen took his children camping or backpacking. Some Saturday nights, after receiving a frantic call from his former wife, he spent cruising the streets looking for his daughter.

Inactive church members are the experts on why they've been absent. Each one knows exactly the reasons he or she is missing. My assumptions or suspicions are inadequate and often wrong. Better to go humbly to learn the inactive person's reasons.

Recognize My Feelings

When I see someone is becoming inactive, a number of feelings stir within me.

Sometimes I'm angry. For instance, I help the Hansens through several life crises. I spend late-night hours counseling them. And as soon as their lives smooth out, they just drift away. It angers me. I had big plans for them. Amy is warm and gracious — the ideal worship greeter. Carl's leadership ability would help our men's ministry. Instead, in spite of my efforts and plans, they're squandering their gifts in the snowmobile club!

Jerry and Kay, on the other hand, made me sad. Their marriage was troubled, and their kids were distancing themselves from the faith. Their son, in particular, had been in trouble with the law and appeared to be on a fast track to big-time hurt. Jerry and Kay were sitting on some time bombs, and they moved away from the church just when they most needed it.

It's difficult, but I need to identify my feelings about inactives. Ironically, that helps me give my full attention to inactives.

Fred gave no indication that he was dissatisfied with our church, but suddenly he began attending another. We had developed a warm relationship, but when I stopped in to see him, he was cool and aloof at first. Eventually, though, he began to tell me that he was dissatisfied with my preaching and wanted to attend a church where the sermons were more to his liking.

When I asked what in my sermons he specifically didn't like, he said, "I just felt I wasn't fed anymore."

That's a response I don't take well. I spend a lot of time on my sermons and feel that there is more meat in them than many people can digest. When someone tells me my sermons don't feed them, it takes great restraint not to defend myself vigorously.

On this occasion, I recognized my rising anger and put it on the shelf for a while. Then I focused on Fred's feelings, trying to see if there was something more.

"Have I offended you in some way?" I asked.

"No," he said, but his facial expression hinted I was on the right track.

"Has someone else offended you?" I continued.

He lowered his eyes and toyed with a paper clip. "Well, yeah, but it's no big deal." He went on to describe an incident in which someone had ignored his input about the budget, implying even that he wasn't spiritually mature. It hit him at a vulnerable time. Since he was, in fact, somewhat unhappy with my preaching, he took it as a convenient out.

That conversation, then, was enough to reopen the door to a good relationship. Had I not recognized my anger and put it aside, I may have focused on the wrong issue. I would have lost a friend and certainly a parishioner. As it is now, he just may come back to us — when he gets hungry for good preaching again!

Show Appreciation

I could hardly believe my ears when Christy, who had been actively involved in the drama team for some time, told me she was ready to quit — not just the drama group but also the church. When I asked why, she recited four or five incidents in which I had ignored or dismissed her suggestions. It seemed others had done the same. She was an inactive ready to happen.

Recovering my composure, I eventually convinced her that these rejections of her ideas were exceptions; we truly valued her.

This experience reawakened me to people's need for recognition and appreciation. Unfortunately, I often fail to notice people who steadily contribute their time and ideas. But I'm learning. In fact, I've asked a few key people in the church to help me spot and creatively acknowledge the valuable ministry of some quiet regulars. Appreciation, I've found, thwarts inactivity.

Respect Inactives' Anger

People who have dropped out have given a good deal of thought to their decision. If they've been offended, they've replayed the offense over and over in their minds. In some instances, they've whipped themselves into a frenzy of self-righteousness. Not coming to church is a dramatic statement of indignation. By the time I see them, inactives are stewing in a deep-rooted problem that will not yield to quick fixes.

Therefore, my first task is to respect the dignity of people who seem to be behaving immaturely. I want to see the offense from their point of view. I want to sense the strength of their emotional storm.

After the Bakers had missed several Sundays, I dropped by to visit. Harley and Eleanor had been offended, but I wasn't sure how. As I sat in their living room, I was determined to listen nondefensively.

In a few moments Harley started in. He was miffed that we didn't sing more traditional hymns. He had grown up on the old hymns, remembered them fondly, and longed for his children to grow up singing them as well.

"We just can't abandon the music the church has sung for hundreds of years," he concluded. "Those hymns mean something to us!"

I was tempted to launch into a defense of contemporary Christian music and explain vigorously the need to reach the new generation, but I checked myself.

"Which hymns do you like best?" I asked.

" 'Rock of Ages,' 'Standing on the Promises,' and 'Blessed Assurance,' are ones we were raised on," said Eleanor.

"Well, I also remember singing those songs on Sunday mornings, Sunday nights, and Wednesday nights," I responded. "They bring back a flood of memories for me, too."

I went on to assure them that others felt as they did. But soon I was able to convince them of the need for new music, especially when I assured them we'd include more of their favorites.

Respecting people's anger, I found, goes a long way toward dissolving that anger.

Take the Inactive's Side

The Hardens had been with our church since our inception thirteen years before. They had struggled with us through cold winters in an inadequate building. We brought blankets and huddled together in that rented building, but such experiences forged bonds among those members.

Then the Hardens began missing a Sunday here and there; eventually they were only hitting a Sunday now and then. They assured me their absence was only due to illness, company, or trips.

When I suspected there was something more, I dropped by to express my concern. We were close and had been through a lot together, so the old times took up a bit of our early conversation.

Then Russ sighed and said, "Those were the good old days. We were all close back then. You could depend on each other. Now, if we miss a few Sundays, the Sunday we return there's some new person greeting us at the door."

As I listened, I found myself mentally accusing Russ and Trish of creating their own problems. Instead of diving in and making new friends, they had pulled back. It seemed as though they were expecting celebrity status from newcomers and then withdrawing when it wasn't accorded.

I composed myself and tried to see the problem from their perspective. I agreed with them; it was a problem. I shared my own concern that our church not lose its personal touch as we grew larger. I also asked them how we could insure that people, new and old, weren't lost in the numbers. Not only did the Hardens offer some good ideas, I couldn't think of anyone better to implement them!

That, in fact, is another strategy I employ when working with inactives.

Channel Inactives' Grievances into Active Ministry

When I found out that one of our single mothers was hurt, disappointed, and ready to leave the church, I stopped by for a visit. She didn't need much prompting.

She began spilling a year and a half of pent-up frustration. She had felt out of place in our family-oriented church. She described the frustrations of trying to make it as a working single mother of a teenage son. It didn't take long for me to feel the helplessness of her plight. And, yes, she had already visited another church in the area intending to find another church home.

I knew she was bright and articulate, but during our conversation I also began to sense that she had some organizational ability. After empathizing with her plight, I asked her to consider doing something positive for herself and the other single mothers in our congregation.

"You're more aware of the needs of single moms than I'll ever be," I began. "You have compassion for others in your situation. Would it help to have a single mothers support group, a group of single moms who could speak openly, and be understood and cared for?"

"Why, yes," she replied.

"Would you consider helping form a single mother's support group?"

"Oh, no," she said, overwhelmed. "I'm not good at that sort of thing. I wouldn't know what to do."

"Jeanette, you've not only described the plight of the single mother in a moving way, but you've also proposed several measures to meet their needs. We'll certainly back you as a church if you'll get together with other single mothers. Will you consider it?"

She did. I described her concerns during the next Sunday morning service, and several single mothers met with her afterward. The following Sunday morning she surveyed people in the church to discover who could offer single mothers some practical skills like plumbing, carpentry, and mechanics. She made her own announcement with a sparkle in her eyes, and our ministry with single mothers was off and running.

Apologize for the Church When It's Wrong

When people have been hurt or offended by the church, extending a simple apology often goes a long way.

For many years I had counseled Sally through marital and parenting woes, financial difficulties, and other personal problems. We had become close, so when her attendance flagged, I stopped by for a visit. The conversation was unusually strained at first, but then she broke forth.

"I loaned the church my big coffee pot for the reception six months ago," she began.

"Okay." I vaguely remembered the incident.

"Well, someone dropped and broke it. No one has said a word since or tried to do anything about it, and all I've got for my generosity is a broken coffee pot."

"Sally, I didn't realize that."

"That's right," she answered, looking as if she'd said something she'd wanted to say for a long time but was slightly embarrassed at finally having said it.

"I'm sorry. I wish I had known. That's certainly not right for you to be stuck with a broken coffee pot."

"And then, several weeks later, I had to move that big piano from upstairs to downstairs. I asked for help during a Sunday morning church service, and no one came. I certainly can't move it by myself, so I had to go out and hire some men to move it. I thought the church was supposed to take care of its own," she concluded with emphasis.

"Sally, I'm sorry at how the church has offended you. It sounds as if it has been a real disappointment."

"Yes, I've felt hurt." She paused, and her demeanor changed. "But I guess I didn't have to sit around stewing in it. After all, I could have come to you with my concerns sooner."

"But sometimes when we're hurt it's difficult to reach out to those who've hurt us. Sally, I'm sorry this has happened to you. You know how much we've been through together and how much Rebecca (my wife) and I love you. I'm sorry you've been hurt." I extended my hand to her. "I don't know what happened with the coffee pot," I continued, "but I can assure you that we'll either get it fixed or get you a new one."

"Oh, it's no big deal, really. It wasn't new. It just seemed as if no one cared."

I also apologized for the church's lack of response to her plea for moving help. But by that time, it didn't seem to matter; she'd said as much, in fact. Her hurt had been healed.

Relieve Unnecessary Guilt

Bob and Jennifer had come to our church as new Christians and had matured through its ministry. But every once in a while they'd make a wrong turn and get sidetracked by financial hardships or marital problems. They'd begin to complain, lay blame, and panic in the face of difficulties.

When they were in a down period, it was difficult to relate with them. They attended church less frequently, and when they came, they were polite but cool.

One night, several months into such a period, I dropped by their home. After we exchanged pleasantries, I plunged into deeper conversation: "You know, guys, it's hard on me when things are not right between us."

They looked at each other with mock surprise. Then Bob said, "What do you mean? There's nothing wrong between us."

"We both know that our relationship is strained. When we talk, I feel as if you're holding up an invisible shield. That hurts. I love you two. You've meant a lot to me."

Jennifer broke in, "You mean a lot to us too, Doug. We don't have anything against you. It's just that we've been going through . . ." She looked at Bob.

"I know you're having some hard times. The economy isn't in good shape, and I know your store is taking it on the chin. It just hurts me to see you hurting alone."

"Well, Doug, we're sick of our problems," sighed Bob. "They get us down. We get depressed and even begin questioning God's love for us. But we don't want to complain. You've heard it all before. Why bother you with it again? We'll be all right someday."

"Do you feel I wouldn't approve of how you're handling yourself?"

"It's pretty obvious that we're letting it pound us into the ground," said Bob. "It's so frustrating. We've learned so much at this church, and we do okay for a while. Then something happens, and we're back in the same pit. We know what we should do, but it's like we're helpless. We fall back into old habits: blaming, looking for an escape, and letting the tension strain our relationship."

"The only thing I'm disappointed in is your blocking me out when you could use a friend," I said. "I'm not thinking, *When will the stupid Hales ever learn!* I know your spiritual strengths and weaknesses. You've come a long way, but you still fall down every once in a while, as does every Christian. I don't look down on you for that."

They exchanged relieved glances at each other. We didn't get into the nitty-gritty of their problems that evening. At that point, they simply needed to receive some grace.

Get the Offended to Talk with Their Offenders

Steve and Katy had stopped attending abruptly early in the summer, but it was well into the fall before I had an opportunity to sit down with them. When I asked about their absences, they pointed to a hectic schedule and sick children as the culprits. It didn't ring true, so I probed more and began to hear a deeper story.

"Well, when that youth group was here for a concert . . . " Katy looked at Steve for permission to continue. He nodded. "We were working on the food committee to put together a meal before the concert. I suggested we have spaghetti and meat sauce since it's easy to prepare and serve. The rest of the committee agreed, and we began planning. But at the next meeting, Margaret showed up and acted like the spaghetti idea was insane."

That didn't surprise me. Margaret can be painfully blunt at times, and sometimes the force of her personality overrides a group.

Steve took up the story. "When Katy came home, she was obviously upset. She felt that Margaret had been rude, and the rest of the committee hadn't cared enough to deal with the issue. They just caved in to Margaret."

"Katy, you must have felt humiliated by Margaret and betrayed by the rest of the committee," I said.

"Yes, I did," Katy replied, choked up. "It really hurt. I still helped with the dinner, but it took the joy out of going to church." Then she sobbed.

"I think I would have felt pretty trampled on myself," I added. "Did you talk with Margaret or any of the others about this?"

Katy said, "Oh, no. After all, the dinner did come off well. I didn't want to cause any trouble."

"But Katy," I replied, "what happened to you is troubling. That's not the way our church should function. We don't want to pull off a good dinner and then have to do a body count later. You were mistreated, and I'm sorry. But I think we can use it, not only to right the wrong you suffered but to learn some important lessons about how to get along as a church."

"What do you mean?"

"I want to get the committee together again and talk about what happened," I answered.

"Oh, no," they said in unison. "We'd prefer not to make trouble. We'll be okay."

"But you're not okay," I responded. "You've had the joy taken from your church experience, you've avoided coming to church, and you're hurt. It's scary to actually talk about a problem. You know that from your marriage. But if you ignore problems, they just build and blow up all over you. It's the same way with church relationships."

Although reluctant, they finally agreed. It took some doing, but we got the committee together. Everyone was uncomfortable when I asked Katy to describe what had happened and how she'd felt. There was some awkward stirring as others listened, and then silence.

Finally Margaret spoke: "That's just like me, taking over and doing it my way." Her husband nodded knowingly as she continued. "I've caused my children no end of trouble by trying to run their lives. It's been hard for me to learn that teenagers need room to maneuver. I guess, unknowingly, I've done the same thing at church. I can't seem to help it. I just take over and assume that everyone will be happier doing it my way."

Then she turned to Katy. "Katy, please forgive me. I didn't mean to offend you." When Katy moved to hug Margaret, there wasn't a dry eye in the house. We spent some time discussing what had happened and how we all could learn from the experience.

It doesn't always work out this nicely, of course. This is a risky strategy that requires a certain level of spiritual maturity among church members. In the case of Steve and Katy, though, I'm happy to report that they returned to active participation and are blossoming as leaders in the church.

Accept Seasonal Inactives

People move to the Rockies for the mountains. They don't move here to attend church. I sometimes forget that. But each season leaves different seats empty. During the ski season there are powder hounds who can't imagine fresh snow without putting the first tracks in it. During the May fly hatch, some fishermen can't tolerate being anywhere but in a river with a fly rod in hand. Summer brings camping, hiking, and backpacking season. The fall brings a zillion hunting seasons. In short, the call of the wild is sometimes stronger than the call of the church.

I used to get self-righteous about those who became inactive during such seasons. When someone would be absent for several Sundays, I'd imagine a spiritual crisis or apostasy. In a panic I'd call on these lost sheep. In some instances, I made my disapproval known, and I damaged a few relationships. I made it difficult for the wandering sinner to come back to the fold after the season was over.

Gradually, I learned that some people's absence was only for a season. If I was patient and forbearing, they usually came back. When looking at their attendance over a period of years, I decided I would rather have people come regularly and then miss a few months each year than offend and lose them forever.

Give Permission to Attend Elsewhere

The Grants were an attractive couple with three children ranging from kindergarten through eighth grade. They were experienced church leaders who had been regular attenders and givers in their previous church. After they moved to our area, they attended our church regularly, joined, and began getting more and more involved. They appeared to be all a pastor could want in church members. Then their attendance flagged.

I visited them when they began missing regularly, but they didn't mention any problems. Then I heard through the grapevine that they were dissatisfied. So I made another call.

Melissa received me as graciously as ever. The kids eagerly showed me their new toys. Finally, I came to the point: "We both know that something is wrong. You're committed Christians, but you've not been coming lately. What's going on?"

They began hesitantly and with the not unusual, "We just don't feel like we're getting fed." I probed and asked what particularly they missed.

Phillip thought for a second and then said, "Your sermons are biblical, and you make good use of humor. But your sermons don't go deep enough for us."

"And we're interested in the deeper Christian life," Melissa interjected. She then named some nationally known preachers to illustrate what she meant. I knew immediately the type of preaching she was talking about, and, frankly, I enjoy such preachers myself.

When I asked them specifically what I should do to satisfy their needs, Phillip said, "We like a lot of cross-referencing in a sermon. You use contemporary illustrations more than you cross-refer from the Bible."

"So you prefer more biblical support and insight for a particular point than contemporary illustration?" I questioned.

They seemed uncomfortable with my assessment but nodded. I kept probing like this until I recognized that the issue went deeper than sermon technique.

"I'm not sure my style of preaching would ever satisfy you," I said. "That's not necessarily an indictment on me or you. I believe people have different needs and even different learning styles. From what you're telling me, I suggest you listen to Mike Nelson at First Baptist, Aspen. I suspect he might better minister to your needs. He's a fine pastor, and they have a good church."

They exchanged an embarrassed look. "We've already visited there," Melissa confessed.

"Well, great!" I replied. "The last thing I want is for you to drop out of church involvement completely. I'm glad you're looking for what you need spiritually. Of course, I'd prefer you didn't leave our church. I've grown attached to you."

They assured me about how much they enjoyed our church and me.

"But, I have no qualms about your being involved in Mike's church," I continued. "He'll take good care of you, and I know you'll be an asset to that church. The important thing is that we remain good friends. I'd hate to think you were leaving our church because you need a different style of preaching but were telling people it's because our church isn't spiritually mature."

"Oh, no," they assured me.

"We're sorry to lose you if you end up elsewhere. But if that's what you choose to do, you'll have our blessing and continued friendship."

"That's our desire, as well," Phillip added. "We were uncomfortable going elsewhere. We thought you'd think we were traitors. We didn't want to be branded as bad guys and have people turn their backs on us."

"Not that we've made that decision," Melissa said. "We're

just praying about it and trying to follow the Lord's will. But your visit has taken the pressure off."

In fact, they did end up going to another church, and they're doing well there. But that's preferable to their (a) going to another church and badmouthing us to justify their decision, or (b) feeling guilty and not going to church at all.

With all these strategies available, one may wonder which is appropriate when and with whom. These many strategies are not, of course, mutually exclusive. More than one can be used with any one inactive. And experience in pastoral care goes a long way toward helping the pastor determine which is best in a particular case.

In the end, however, there are no hard-and-fast rules, because pastoral care to inactives is finally, like painting, an art. These strategies are merely the colors on our ministry palette.

After a spiritual turning point, a person needs to understand both the glory of an event and the dynamics of the ongoing process of spiritual growth.

— Paul Anderson

Nurturing the Revitalized

P ostpartum blues hit more than new mothers.

Our congregation's worship leader and I helped lead music at a praise service for a church convention. Scores of people, some with tears, had come up afterward to tell us how they had appreciated worship. When I returned to my hotel room, I found a note from my colleague, saying, "Praise God. Jesus was glorified this evening. Stand against discouragement — and have a good sleep."

The next day I asked what he meant. He said, "I often battle discouragement after a spiritual high, and yesterday I was flying."

This is not only a personal issue; it's also pastoral. My parishioners enjoy spiritual highs from time to time — at seminars and retreats, in worship, and in dramatic answers to prayer. Those events transform people's hearts and lives.

Yet coming off the mountain can be painful. Ask Peter, James, and John after they had seen their leader transfigured. Peter felt compelled to stretch the moment into a millennium. Do you blame him? On the mountain the disciples probably felt they could invade hell. In the valley they failed at casting out a demon.

So, when God has moved specially in people's lives, what's the pastor's next move? After people have experienced the power and love of God on Sunday, what do we say about Monday? When friends have life-changing encounters, how can the gains of God's special activity be preserved?

Put Events in Their Place

The first step is, through preaching and teaching, to put such events in perspective.

Sometimes people need an event to jar them loose from encrusted habits or set them on a new path. A gathering following a service, an altar call, or a fresh commitment at a retreat is such an event. Yet, by their very nature they are uncommon experiences. They are part of the way a gracious God deals with us, but they are exceptional.

People often come to us looking for an event, a quick spiritual high. It may have taken twenty years to develop the anxiety they live with, but they want it gone in an hour. I don't blame them. I battled acute insecurity in seminary. I lacked the simple confidence to stand in class to speak. I was unsure of my relationships with fellow students. I dearly wished I could have been lifted out of that pit.

As tempting as it may be to seek events, however, I have to remind myself and my people that we cannot depend upon a series of events to bring us into maturity, any more than a baby needs multiple births to learn how to walk. Instead of waiting for the next "Spirit fix," we need to learn how to put one foot in front of the other. There's nothing dramatic about walking, but it gets you there, little by little.

We had a high-powered speaker come to our church a few years ago. One advantage of an evangelist is that he can stir up activity that would take the local shepherd months to generate. But the strength is also a liability. He may abort what is not ready for birth. He may force an event when a process is needed. We had some events that night: dynamic speaker, dramatic words, people visibly moved by the power of the Spirit. But I noticed over the next few months that people found no long-term help. They went back to the same old spiritual struggles.

Another time, a young man was battling with fears he could not explain. He came for counseling several times, hoping for deliverance. We believe in deliverance when appropriate, but behind this man's fear was pride that grew out of a performance-oriented upbringing. The script had been written by Dad, and he was following it closely.

As the counselor listened to and prayed with the young man, he finally suggested to him that his life was like a wagon going west. Freedom was coming for the young man, but it would be a slow and gradual process. That wasn't exactly what the man wanted to hear, but time validated the word. His was a problem not of the Devil but of the flesh, and one cannot exorcise the flesh, only offer it as a living sacrifice.

In short, people need a proper mindset to understand the difference between a spiritual experience and spiritual growth.

Progress Through Process

Besides putting events in perspective, I also need to remind myself and my people of the biblical dynamics of spiritual growth.

• *Truth is always tested.* After Jesus was baptized and filled with the Spirit, he was directed by the Spirit into the wilderness. The wilderness in Scripture often represents a place of testing, where God tries us to prove us, and Satan tempts us to defeat us. How we act after heaven opens up (and hell breaks loose) is critical to our spiritual growth.

Jerry called the day after meeting God at a retreat. His prayers that the Holy Spirit would be evident in his life had been answered. But the next day doubts set in; he wondered if the experience was no more than a passing emotional high. When I simply explained that Satan always challenges what God does, Jerry flexed his spiritual muscles and stood his ground.

• *Growth is cyclical.* Growth in faith is hardly a straight ascending line. Although sometimes it feels like a jagged ascending line — where our growth is interrupted by brief falls — most of the time it's more like an ascending series of loops. Before we make progress, we often have to go back over old territory. In doing so, it may seem like we're going backwards when we're actually going deeper.

For example, Barbara's mind was nearly gone when she came to us. She was desperate. She said that something had to happen immediately, or she would go crazy. I assured her the Lord could restore her mind but that it might take a while. In fact, it took longer than I expected, but after months of people praying with and caring for her in a small group, she began to smile, laugh, and reason again.

After five months of progress, however, she came into the office, worried. "I'm not getting better," she said. "My mind is still a mess, I'm still not free, and I am right where I started." I smiled because the change in her was obvious to all who knew her, and I told her so. Then I went over the diagram above with her, and she walked out with a light step. She just needed to know that God was at work, that she could trust the process, however slow and cyclical.

• *Fruit is developed.* Spiritual fruit is not given; it is grown. God's gifts, including the gifts of salvation and the Holy Spirit, can be received in an instant. God's goal for us, however, is that we conform to the image of his Son and produce the fruit of the Spirit: love, joy, peace, patience, and the like. And that takes time.

Recently, through our relationship with Alcoholics Anonymous, drug users and long-time alcoholics have come to our church. Most of them realize it will take time to be fully healed, but others are hoping the pastor will fix them immediately. I tell them,

"Stay with us, and let us love you back into health. I can't tell you how long it will take, but if you stick it out, the Lord can heal you."

● *I have changed; life has not.* I remember riding high after going forward at a Billy Graham meeting at the Los Angeles Coliseum. I expected all of life to change after my beautiful experience. I wanted all my relationships suddenly to be improved. I hoped everyone would be nice from then on. When the emotions were rubbed off by reality, however, I was back to the humdrum of life.

I had failed to realize that what had changed was me, not life. I needed the Bible's wisdom that "if any man is in Christ, he (not everybody else) is a new creation."

The day after a wonderful retreat often hits us with the dull thud of reality. Instead of having our devotions under a pine tree, we awake to three screaming kids in the next room. We soaked up the love of God for three wonderful days; now we are expected to balance the checkbook, make four difficult phone calls, and service a faulty washing machine.

Teaching people about the *process* of faith can help them handle with maturity the disparity between mountaintop highs and life in the valley.

Shape the Event Appropriately

How we minister to people *during* spiritual events can also help the process of spiritual growth. When we recognize that a service or retreat may lead to a mountaintop experience, we can shape it so that it has lasting effects.

In particular, I've found Jesus' parable of the sower (Mt. 13:1–23) a handy guide in such times.

● *Aim for the mind also.* Ministry that emphasizes emotion at the expense of understanding will merely provide breakfast for Satan — the bird that eats the seed that falls on hard ground in the parable. It is more important to help people understand what is happening than just to create a happening.

If during a powerful event a person says, "I don't under-stand," we should resist saying, "That's all right; just receive it by faith." Lasting faith must be built on understanding; it's not a leap in the dark.

• *Shape the event for the long-term.* The second group in the parable respond enthusiastically, but they do not last when trouble sets in. The emotion of joy is an appropriate response to the working of the Spirit, but a ministry that makes people feel that they will live happily ever after may be preparing them for heaven but not for earth.

Thus during the event itself, it's helpful to prepare people for the long road ahead, to remind them of the difference between the mountain and the valley, between triumph and testing, between momentary ecstasy and patient sanctification.

Remembering the long-term also means respecting the history and personality of the church when planning and leading an event. One woman who led a retreat for us came asking questions about our congregation, about our traditions and our expectations. She invited our leaders to participate in her services. During the services she gave me a prominent role of anointing with oil those who requested it.

In contrast with the visiting evangelist I described above, she not only led an exciting spiritual event, her ministry also bore lasting results. For example, one young man who was healed of back problems during her ministry with us gave himself to Christ, and has continued on in strong faith since.

• *Remember repentance.* The third group in the parable functioned well until the word was choked out by worldly cares. During glorious spiritual events, I must also be willing to remind people of worldly cares that may hinder them when they come off the mountain.

Frankly, I'd rather bask in the wonderful moment. But glory without the Cross isn't Christ's way. If I'm interested in sustaining my people's growth, I must also challenge them at such times.

One Lenten service a woman in the congregation shared a simple insight she received: she sensed the Lord drawing near to us that night. I seldom give altar calls, but after this word, I did so. I wanted people not only to know the joy of Christ's presence, but also to open themselves to the Lord in new ways, perhaps in ways that would require new humility and trust.

• *Let God move as he will.* The fourth group in the parable responded to the word and experienced supernatural dividends. Naturally, that is what we want to see happen. But sometimes, in our anxiety for spiritual highs, we try to make them occur prematurely.

To say, for example, "God is moving tonight" or "I feel the Lord in this place" may be accurate, or it may simply express the leader's desire that God do something.

At one of our services, a visiting evangelist announced how much he felt the Lord was doing in our midst. I had my doubts. In the days before the service, as I entertained and spoke with him, I noticed that he usually talked less about God and more about his ministry. His observation that God was in our midst struck me as anxious hope more than quiet confidence.

It might make the minister look better if everyone agrees that the night was powerful, but such language cannot make it happen.

Jesus' approach was just the opposite. When moved by a powerful event, he urged people not to speak about it. He didn't announce the mighty works of God; he simply allowed them to happen through him, when and where God willed.

What to Do Back in the Valley

How can we take people from the event into the process so that we preserve the gains? I've found three elements go a long way toward that end.

• *Follow up.* During one Sunday service, we encouraged people struggling with addictions and unhealthy habits to come forward. Eighteen people responded. So we contacted all eighteen people to see if we could link them with someone who could provide ongoing counsel. They were thankful to know we weren't operating a "one-night stand" but would stick with them.

Pastors cannot get personally involved in all the follow-up, but they can nurture the kind of spiritual network in a church that makes ongoing follow-up possible. That means building the expectation that ministry belongs to everyone in the congregation, helping people discover their gifts, and giving them confidence and opportunities to use them.

Specifically, we've trained ten of our members to be available to pray and counsel with people after services and special events. Such people have given counsel and support to many new Christians and troubled believers who wouldn't have made it without such help. One divorcée whose spiritual crisis we had followed up said, "I don't see how I could have made it without the support of people in the congregation."

• *Support support groups.* In a crisis, Marsha came for counseling. She had known the Lord for many years, but she still battled with a low self-image. She found it hard to receive love from others, though she was a thoughtful and caring person who encouraged others with kind words and creative notes. She eventually shared her story with me — her abuse as a child and the shame that clouded her life, making her feel like dirt. Her tearful confession was a momentary high, a release from her past.

That might have remained a momentary experience had not a support group for sexually abused women given her courage to move steadily through her pain to healing. In the group she was able to share her background and receive loving support. Two years later she was able to say to the leader, "I don't need to come anymore. I have received what I need. Thank you."

• *Help people affirm their victories.* One good way to cement victories is to make daily confessions of faith. Language has a way of firming up new trust. So, we often give people statements of faith that we encourage them to recite at least once a day, affirmations such as:

"There is therefore now no condemnation. I don't condemn myself, and I don't condemn anyone else."

"I stand fast in the freedom that Christ gave me, and I allow others the same freedom."

"I am a child loved by God. Therefore, I love myself."

This is especially helpful at thwarting the natural tendency to live in the nostalgia of yesterday's blessings. Jesus taught us to pray, "Give us this day our daily bread." The psalmist wrote that God is "a very present help in trouble" and that "his mercies are new every morning." We give people affirmations of faith not only to cement past blessings, but also to reveal new ones in the lifelong process of Christian growth.

● *Reveal your own struggles.* When the scenery shifts after visiting the mountaintop, and people find themselves in the valley, they need to know they are not alone.

I've found that the more honest I can be about my struggles, the more free members are in discussing theirs. And that helps them walk patiently until victory comes again.

I find many opportunities to talk like this with people one to one. Recently on vacation, I visited a former member who now is a leader in another church. He asked me to pray with him because his spiritual life seemed unusually dry. When I told him about some of my struggles in the deserts of faith, it was a great encouragement to him.

Caring for the revitalized means helping them understand both the glory of an event and the dynamics of the ongoing process of spiritual growth. Birth is an event, growth a process — spiritually and physically.

"As you have received Christ," wrote Paul, "so walk in him." Receiving Christ or a new infusion of the Spirit may help people leap for joy. But ironically, that's just when we need to teach them how to walk.

PART THREE

Practicing Care

It's not saying the right things but listening in the right way that's crucial to personal visitation.

— Doug Self

CHAPTER EIGHT

The Art of Pastoral Listening

I would see Ed and Elaine at church or in the community. They were friendly; I was friendly. But we didn't get into extended conversations. I had heard they were having serious marital problems. The wife, in fact, had inquired about counseling with me, but the husband had been restive.

I knew I wasn't going to take the initiative. At best, they would demand months of counseling. At worst, I feared that I couldn't help them at all.

So on we went: I knew, and they knew, and we all pretended

that we didn't know. I sometimes felt guilty for not visiting them. Nonetheless, I put it off — for years.

My pastoral responsibilities include visitation. In fact, I've experienced some success in this part of ministry. But I still find myself apprehensive about visiting people.

Why? Because I'm afraid I won't say the right thing at the right time. Maybe I won't say the appropriate word to calm the grieving widow or counter the objection of the unbeliever, or know what to say during seemingly pointless conversation.

I can overcome such fear in one of two ways. I can learn to say always the right thing at the right time, but let's face it, that's never going to happen. Or I can realize that it's not saying the right things but listening in the right way that's crucial to personal visitation.

I'll take the latter, and not because it's easier. Actually, good listening can be grueling. But when I focus on listening to another, it takes the pressure off me. I become less concerned about me and more about the person I'm listening to. I don't come as an expert ready to spew forth, but as a learner seeking to discover.

When that's my attitude, visitation is not daunting, although it remains a challenge. Here, then, are some things I've learned about listening.

Pastors Are Half Listeners

A study cited in Larry Barker's *Listening Behavior* (Spectra) shows that pastors spend 45 percent of their time listening and only 30 percent speaking. Reading takes up 16 percent of our time and writing another 9.

For pastors, then, nearly half of each week is taken up with simply listening to people. We have a variety of opportunities to listen: brief encounters with people in the hallways of the church, phone calls, committee meetings, counseling, and especially visits with our people.

Consequently, listening has become a crucial ministry skill. When I do it well, it makes a difference.

Bill and Eloise had been attending our church for some time

before I had a chance to visit them. They were quiet and reserved, yet I suspected swirling currents behind their smiles. When I finally visited them one evening, they were reluctant to talk honestly. But when they saw I was genuinely interested in them, that I wasn't going to dish out easy answers, they began to tell me their story, piece by piece.

Bill had lost his job. Months turned into years as his job search proved futile. So he worked as a laborer for less than a quarter of his former salary. Then they learned that their middle son had cancer. Medical bills started piling higher, and their son's condition continued to deteriorate until he died. They were emotionally and financially drained.

Still Bill worked on, making an honest effort to provide for his family and pay the bills. As we talked late into the evening, they told me they had just received word that foreclosure proceedings were being set in motion on their house.

Bill and Eloise weren't asking for explanations or charity or sympathy. Naturally reticent people, they hadn't disclosed the inner workings of their lives to others. They were hardy stock and didn't want to complain. Yet once they opened up, they clearly were eager to have someone listen to their story.

Listening: Focused Mental Attention

I've had to develop two crucial and, for me, unnatural skills to become an effective listener: focused mental attention and attending physical behavior.

First, I had to learn to focus on what the other person says. Understanding another person accurately requires me to devote all my mental energies. That isn't easy, because as I listen I can easily fall into several habits that distract my attention away from the other person. So I regularly remind myself of the following guidelines before and as I listen.

1. *Defer judgment.* Being, as I am, in the business of teaching people right from wrong and truth from error, it's difficult sometimes to listen to people's stories without judging them. But when I start judging, I start thinking about what they should do to change,

and I stop thinking about what, in fact, they are telling me. Instead, I try to suspend judgment, no matter what I'm inclined to believe about the person.

I met Mike through a community organization we both attended. Although he didn't attend church, he was interested in spiritual matters, which prompted several prolonged conversations. He told me he used drugs. He was also sexually active, and his good looks guaranteed a steady supply of partners. However, about a year previously he had begun to question his lifestyle. He began to think of his drug friends as "real creeps" but also wondered aloud if he wasn't like them.

He said indiscriminate sex was a compulsion, and he'd begun to hate himself for not being able to stop. Although he enjoyed the experiences, he loathed what he was becoming and how impersonally he was treating his partners. But he wouldn't stop.

In short, Mike lived a lifestyle contrary to Christian teachings. At this point in our conversations, it took a special effort not to judge but to keep listening.

One weekend he climbed one of the mountain peaks in our area. He told me later that taking in the view, he found himself crying out, "God, help me. Help me to be different!" This was a new experience for Mike since he had not grown up in a religious home. He didn't recall feeling anything, however, and chalked it up as a failed effort at reform.

As the months went on, however, he began to recognize the operation of a moral standard within himself that gently pointed out the right and wrong of his actions.

Mike still had plenty of questions. His active mind was constantly probing, trying to understand, for instance, God's role in the universe, in its creation and present operation. He'd never entertained the idea of creation before.

As he unwound his story over weeks of conversations, I continued to listen. Although I told him about the difference Christ could make in his life, I didn't unload all my biblical answers. Those would have to come slowly. First, I needed to know more about Mike, his religious experiences, his conclusions about life.

At one point in our conversations he said, "You're one person I could tell this to who won't think less of me." It was important to Mike that he be able to talk about his spiritual interests and questions without feeling put down. As it was, Mike and I had many conversations about spiritual matters, and before he moved away from our area, he was becoming increasingly willing to consider a relationship with Jesus Christ.

2. *Preempt preoccupations.* Pastors usually have dozens of things demanding their attention. Unfinished business is my constant companion. At any given time a pastor can be mulling a half-finished sermon, planning a program, stewing over budget problems, fretting the unresolved problems of various church members. It's easy to be preoccupied.

So when I begin a pastoral visit, I focus on the importance of that personal encounter. I consciously put aside my other concerns. *I will be totally present with this person during the time we have together,* I think to myself. If I don't do something deliberate like that, my preoccupations may cause me to miss things.

Once in a staff meeting I excitedly related an idea I had heard from another associate, Dan. It was well received, but after the meeting Suzy, our administrative assistant, drew me aside.

"Doug," she said, "don't you remember that I offered that same idea at a previous meeting?"

"No," I replied, searching my mind.

"I brought up the same thing at our brainstorming session. At the time you didn't respond, and I thought you didn't like the idea."

"Uh," I stammered, "I don't remember what you said." She described the conversation in more detail, and I faintly recalled her contribution, but at the time I had been preoccupied.

"When you were so excited about the idea tonight," she continued, "and reported it as Dan's, I was hurt."

Now, numbed by my oversight, I apologized for my insensitivity and reminded myself to put aside distractions deliberately before I enter into conversations.

3. *Avoid premature solutions.* People look to pastors for

answers. I too often feel obliged to provide them quickly and easily. Quick answers, however, often leave out critical factors and shut down further communication. Even when the quick answer is correct, it may be rejected because people don't feel their problems are taken seriously. No wonder: I cannot listen fully when I am engaged in mentally formulating answers.

So, I make sure I've listened for a while and taken in sufficient information before I dare interject a solution or insight.

Jim and Susan were struggling in their marriage. They fought often, and it usually ended up coming back to one particular issue: a failed business venture of Jim's. And every time, they returned to square one with defensiveness, recriminations, and accusations. Jim would try to explain why he had failed. Susan, upon hearing the repeated explanations, thought Jim was merely trying to justify himself. So, they would argue for hours before giving up, exhausted and frustrated.

In one counseling session, such an argument erupted. After listening for some time, I ventured an observation. "Jim, I think you're desperately pleading for Susan to accept you and not condemn you as a failure for the rest of your life. Is that correct?"

Jim looked surprised. "Yes, I feel like a failure as a husband and a provider. I feel worthless." He dropped his head in his hands and sobbed.

Susan put a hand on his knee. "Jim, I don't think you're a failure. That was just one unfortunate decision."

At that point, they stopped blaming and started talking. A premature "You two need to forgive each other" would not have accomplished much. Patient and attentive listening, however, helped me see the real issue more clearly.

4. *Absorb accusations.* Pastors are convenient targets for other people's religious frustrations. I often find myself put on the spot, the brunt of accusations against God, Christianity, and the church.

My first inclination is to defend the faith, because people are attacking things dear to me. But even though apologetics may be in order in some conversations, defensiveness never is. When I become defensive, I start mentally mustering arguments to unravel my opponent. At that point, I am no longer attending to the other person. Then again, if I keep listening *through* the attack, I usually am able to offer some help.

When I stopped in to check on Gary and Mindy, I sensed something amiss. Instead of the usual friendly banter, nervousness and tension hung in the air. After a few minutes of stilted conversation, Gary finally spoke: "It's Kathy (their daughter). We found out that she's been doing some drugs."

Mindy then broke into sobs. "How could this happen to us? Where did we go wrong?" They had endured other blows lately, but this overwhelmed her. "I don't understand how God could let this happen."

Gary comforted Mindy and explained to me, "A lot of things have been building up. We're just tired of fighting it. We're exhausted. This is too much."

I went over and put my arms around both of them. I told them how I felt for them and how overwhelming it must be for them. Mindy stiffened and said, "Yes, it's just too much this time! We've tried to do right, and look what happened." She was angry with God, with the church, with life.

When people fault God, I'm tempted to step in as his defense attorney. But this time I listened without much comment. I tried to discover the particulars of their story. By my posture and words, I tried to indicate I wouldn't argue with them or judge them. I just sat and tried to feel their anguish with them.

Within several weeks, after they'd had time to gain some distance from the crisis, they sought me out for help. They realized their attitudes were causing friction between them and strangling their spiritual vitality. They were then able to ask for help and listen themselves.

Listening: Attending Behavior

The other essential listening skill is attending behavior, the nonverbal parts of conversation: eye contact, facial expressions, and body posture.

Attending behavior, for all its seeming passivity, is a powerful skill. In one experiment, six college students were trained in attending behavior. Then a visiting lecturer, not known for his dynamic lecturing, was invited to class. The lecturer was tied to his notes and used no gestures, and his voice droned on in a monotone.

At a prearranged signal, the students began to evidence attending behavior: they riveted their eyes on the lecturer, leaned forward in their chairs, took on intent expressions. Within thirty seconds the lecturer gestured for the first time, his voice inflection became more dynamic, and his presentation more lively (from Robert Bolton, *People Skills,* Prentice-Hall, 1979).

Attending behavior is a powerful motivational tool. It draws people out. It lets them know they are being taken seriously. But attending behavior is subtle, so it's something I have to pay attention to, lest I communicate the wrong thing.

Some time ago, I was eating breakfast at a local restaurant with a friend. A man walked to our table and asked, "Are you Doug Self, the pastor?" When I said I was, he sat down and began telling us about his Christian commitment and plans to move to our area.

After a few minutes the man left, and my friend asked, "Why were you so aloof, so hostile to a new person in the community?"

"Aloof and hostile?" I asked, "What do you mean? I visited with him. I talked with him."

Then my friend pointed out that I had taken a body position that faced 90 degrees away from him, folded my arms, and looked out the window during parts of the conversation.

I was surprised. I knew I was vaguely uncomfortable with the man, but I thought I had been gracious to him.

As I thought about it afterward, I realized what had happened. I have been burned by many people who come into our community, talk a good religious line, but end up causing problems in the church and community. Although I thought I was communicating acceptance to the man, my body was signaling what I felt inside: that I pegged him as potential trouble and hoped he would stay away.

Over the years, I have worked on my inherent prejudice

against such people. And when I am aware that distrust is stirring within me, I deliberately monitor my body language. Sometimes such people have ulterior motives, but first I want to give them the benefit of the doubt, with my words and my body posture.

Good Questions Show Good Listening

Robert L. Montgomery, who leads seminars in executive skills and has written *Listening Made Easy* (Amacom, 1981), has polled his seminar attendees over the years, asking them what signals a good listener. The ten most common characteristics mentioned are:

1. Looks at me while I'm speaking.
2. Questions me to clarify what I'm saying.
3. Shows concern by asking questions about my feelings.
4. Repeats some things I say.
5. Doesn't rush me.
6. Is poised and emotionally controlled.
7. Responds with a nod of the head, a smile, or a frown.
8. Pays close attention.
9. Doesn't interrupt me.
10. Keeps on the subject until I've finished my thoughts.

I was impressed that two of the top three characteristics have to do with the ability to ask questions. A good listener, it seems, is also someone who asks good questions.

As another pastor put it, "What the scalpel is to the surgeon, the question is to the pastoral counselor. . . . The good pastor is one who knows what to ask and what not to ask, plus has a feel for timeliness" (Russell Dicks, *Pastoral Work and Personal Counseling*, MacMillan).

So over the years I've worked on asking good questions, ones that will both keep the discussion on target and help me know more about the person with whom I talk.

Subject-Changing Questions

Pastors simply don't have time to sit through extensive conversations with everyone. So sometimes, when it seems appropriate, I must gently nudge the conversation toward spiritual concerns.

That must be done naturally and nonintrusively, of course. A good rule of thumb is to change the subject only when others begin to run out of steam on their original topic.

For example, John is excitedly telling me about a remodeling project, going into great detail. I grow restless and want to get on to spiritual matters. While he's between sentences, I may be tempted to insert, "That's great, John. But how's the remodeling of your Christian life going?"

That would be jolting, inappropriately timed. If I can't gracefully move the conversation along, then I'd just as soon hear people out on subjects that are dear to them. Even if we can't talk about spiritual concerns on that visit, at least I will show interest and respect for them.

At the right time, however, directive questions can link spiritual matters to the person's subject of conversation. For example, if the other person is talking about childhood, I might ask, "What memories of church do you have from childhood?" and "What did you most enjoy about your childhood church experience?"

If the person is talking about family, I might ask, "Where in your family life do you feel the church could be most helpful now?" or "What family problems. do you now face that you could use some help with?"

If the person is mentioning a struggle, I might ask, "What feelings have you most struggled with in this situation?" or "Have you found God to be helpful in your situation?"

I use gentle, subject-probing questions to discover background, feelings, attitudes, interests, questions, and needs.

Subject-Probing Questions

These questions help people focus on the subject under discussion. They allow people to sort through their experiences and analyze their reasons and feelings. They also help me learn key facts.

These questions are not that difficult to formulate. I simply ask, in one form or another, the classic journalistic questions: "Who?" "What?" "When?" "Where?" "Why?" and "How?"

For example, if I'm talking with someone who expresses hostility about something, I might ask one or more of the following:

- "When did you begin to feel this way?"
- "What experience has most influenced you to feel this way?"
- "Why do you think you responded that way to that experience?"
- "Who has been helpful to you in this situation?"
- "Where do you think all this is heading?"
- "How have you tried to handle this so far?"

Such questions help me understand people and help people understand themselves. As a result, people often discover previously hidden inconsistencies or underlying assumptions.

Elaine was having difficulty releasing bitterness toward some past business associates. Not only had they cheated her financially, they had also prospered while Elaine had struggled to make ends meet. Now, ten years later, the hurts remained fresh and painful. Elaine became especially prickly when she saw her former business associates in town.

When we talked, I let her express her rage for some time.

"You know what really hurts?" she sobbed at one point. "Seeing them prosper while I've barely made it. It's just not fair. I'm the one who tried to live the Christian principles. They're the ones who violated God's will. Why would God prosper them? It's just not fair, and it's driving a wedge between me and God."

Then I felt it was time to probe.

"It sounds like some of your theology says, 'God should punish the bad and bless the good.' Is that right?"

"Well," she stammered, "I guess I know in my head that

probably isn't right, but that's sure the way I'm feeling."

"Let me dig a little more," I said. "Do you believe that God deliberately made them rich and kept you poor?"

She thought for a moment. "No, I don't think God has actively been working against me financially."

"But as you read the circumstances, does it seem that God may be responsible for your poverty and for their prosperity?"

"Well, yes. My experience certainly indicates that. But I don't suppose that's what the Bible actually teaches," she surmised.

From there we were able to have a fruitful discussion, at the end of which she began to see that rather than blaming God for her situation, she could depend on God in her situation.

As I mentioned, listening skills can be employed in many facets of ministry. But they're especially helpful in home visitation. They not only help make those visits more meaningful, they also make those visits more possible. I don't put off calls as much when I realize that it's not what I say but what the other person says that makes the difference.

An essential step in preparing people to minister is to encourage them to take risks, to go places where they will fail unless God intervenes.

— Bruce Larson

CHAPTER NINE

Risking Lay Ministry

Every pastor I know affirms the priesthood of all believers and preaches that every Christian is called to ministry, including the ministry of providing pastoral care for one another. But most also admit there's a big gap between the actual and desired level of lay ministry.

One reason for this, I believe, is that releasing people to minister involves risks, both for pastor and people. For the pastor, it means giving up control, shedding the "I can handle it" image. For lay people, it means taking on responsibilities bigger than they've ever imagined, tackling situations in which they might not have all the answers, providing pastoral care when they seem to have few resources. And that's scary.

I once had the chance to ask the Swiss physician Paul Tournier, "How do you help your patients get rid of their fears?"

"I don't," he said. "Everything that's worthwhile in life is scary. Choosing a school, choosing a career, getting married, having kids — all those things are scary. If it is not fearful, it is not worthwhile."

As I mentioned earlier, it's vital to get lay people involved in ministry because, among other reasons, it's the most effective way to give pastoral care to the congregation and community. But to get more lay people into ministry, we'll have to take some risks — and help our people to do the same. In fact, during my years of ministry, I've discovered four principles that help me do that wisely and effectively.

Stepping Off the Pedestal

If lay people are going to minister, they have to see their leaders in ministry situations — both on the giving end and the receiving end.

My natural inclination is to "do unto others" but discourage people from "doing unto me," because I'd rather not feel indebted. I have to resist the desire to look competent and secure at all times. Sometimes the desire to seem self-sufficient is my own, but sometimes other people want me to live up to that image. Either way, if lay people are going to minister effectively, I must resist being conformed to that image.

Sometimes after a Sunday sermon, someone will say, "That was a challenging message."

I'll say, "But how do we apply that? What I said is true, and I believe it, but I'm not sure how to live it out. You've got to help me." The final application of a sermon rests on me as well as on the congregation.

Throughout the Gospels, Jesus seems to find ways to use his own needs to bless people. To Zacchaeus he said, "Can you feed thirteen guys at your house? We're hungry." Zacchaeus was eager to oblige, and his life was changed by that lunch.

To an outcast woman at a well Jesus said, "Can you get me a drink? I don't have a cup."

The night before his trial and crucifixion, he asked three friends to keep him company. He said, "I'm scared. Come pray with me."

That's our example.

One Sunday afternoon at my last church, I was reading the paper, when suddenly my brain felt as if it was being stabbed by a dozen ice picks. With the help of some toothache medicine, I managed to make it through the night. The next day the doctor gave me the diagnosis — shingles — and $125 worth of prescriptions.

By Wednesday, the night we were beginning a class on lay ministry, it wasn't any better, so I said, "This is our first session on 'becoming a minister,' and I'm in need of pastoral care right now. At the end of class, some elders are going to come and pray for me and anoint me with oil. You can all see how that healing ministry is done."

At 9 o'clock when I finished teaching, the elders still hadn't shown up. One of the class members said, "Well, why can't *we* pray for you?"

"Why not?" I said.

One woman found some suntan oil in her purse, and the whole class gathered around me, anointed me with the oil, and prayed. Just as they finished, the elders arrived, and we prayed all over again. Two days later, I was well.

In the next Sunday's sermon, I mentioned having shingles, how two groups of people had prayed, and how God had taken the pain away. The next week a man wrote me, "I want to thank you for being in the pulpit last Sunday just a week after you got shingles. I know that nobody gets rid of shingles in a week. I know God healed you. I've never seen a miracle before. Now, with my own eyes, I believe I've seen one."

I would never choose to have shingles, but God used it to demonstrate his healing power and to bless people. Part of the blessing, in this case, was that people in the class saw *they* could minister with confidence.

Yet another way to encourage lay ministry is by having lay people tell publicly what God was doing in their lives. For instance, once I led a Session retreat at which three elders launched the first night by telling their remarkable stories. One man told about having two of his daughters killed in separate car accidents, one involving a drunken driver. He and his wife have survived, and the miracle is, they're not bitter. By the end of his story, many were tearful.

A second man had been through a divorce. He is now happily remarried with wonderful kids and a powerful ministry, but he talked about the pain of divorce. "You never get over the pain. The pain is always there."

Next a schoolteacher, a woman in her thirties, told her story: "I never thought I'd be this old and still be unmarried." She shared her disappointment and her reliance on God. It was a holy moment.

All the next morning and into the afternoon, the storytelling continued, this time in groups of seven. Everyone got to share his or her story — "This is where I'm coming from . . . where God found me . . . where I am now . . . where my pain is . . . where God is leading me."

People need role models for that kind of vulnerability — pastors and church leaders who will risk sharing their pain and their dreams. Such modeling shows people that ministry begins in weakness, not strength. That, in turn, encourages them to speak about their own pain and releases them to minister to one another with less fear of inadequacy.

Limiting the Essential Qualifications

It's normal to fear putting ministry into the hands of lay people, because they haven't proven themselves. But we can put so many requirements in the way that people never reach out to others in Jesus' name.

I believe people need a relationship with the living Christ before they can minister, but that's about the only qualification.

I don't like to have an elaborate screening process, but people must answer three crucial questions affirmatively before I believe they are qualified to minister in the power of the Holy Spirit.

1. *Do you have a relationship with Jesus?* The church is full of people who believe in Jesus but have never met him. The relevant question isn't, "Do you believe Jesus died on the cross?" The Devil believes that much. The question Jesus asks his disciples is, "Do you love me?"

2. *Will you love one another as I have loved you?* is also a question Jesus asked his disciples.

I'm sure that wasn't easy. We can imagine the disciples muttering, "Love those eleven guys? But they're crude, rude, bossy, and pushy."

Nevertheless, Jesus asks, "Are you willing to love this family of believers I have put you with?" Willingness to love and work with other Christians indicates our commitment to discipleship. To me this means being willing to be part of a small group of believers who know me as well as I know myself.

In new members' classes at my last church, for instance, we tried to reproduce the experience of community Jesus had with the Twelve. For part of each session, people met in small groups. Some didn't like that and after the first night never come back. That's okay. I said, "We believe in *koinonia* here, in community, the body of Christ. If you're not ready to be a part of that, then this isn't where you belong."

Those who said yes to community found in their small groups support and accountability for their lives and ministries.

3. *Will you go into the world in my name?* If we're willing to go as God's representative to any place and anyone, God will place us in ministry. I think one of the big myths about ministry is that Jesus sends us only to hard places. A poet once was asked how he wrote poetry. "It's either easy or impossible," he confided. "You can't do it by hard work." That's true of Christian ministry: if it's hard work and nothing else, it's probably not God's place for you.

Some of those places where Jesus sends people look hard only because I couldn't do what people there are doing. For instance, I couldn't do what Mother Teresa did in Calcutta. But God hasn't asked me to do that.

What he has asked me to do, I can do — even if it seems intimidating at first. And what's more, as I do it, I find joy in it.

Each Friday, a group of Christian men in Seattle visits prisoners in a maximum-security facility. They have to leave at 4 A.M. and sometimes don't get back until midnight. They don't feel like martyrs; they're not complaining. They love meeting with the prisoners. They go because that's where they want to be.

I know a nurse who decided to spend her weekends working with AIDS patients. Not everyone would choose that, but she found satisfaction in it.

So I tell people, "Don't assume God will send you to the hardest place. Start with those places where you would *like* to make a difference for Christ." That changes the whole concept of missions in the church.

Encouraging Risk Taking

Although parishioners often start their ministries with what they would *like* to do, we want to encourage them to stretch. People accomplish more when they risk more.

Jesus sent out his disciples — not just the Twelve, but also the seventy — prematurely, they may have felt. "I am sending you out like sheep among wolves," he said. He told them to heal the sick, to cast out evil spirits, to preach the kingdom of God.

He sent them out two by two. Alone, they would have been too scared; they wouldn't have taken the risk.

Jesus shows us that an essential step in preparing people to minister is to encourage them to take risks, to go places where they may fail unless God intervenes.

A few years ago, Carolyn, a deacon in the church I served, came to me with a concern. "I'm a closet alcoholic. I'm dry now, thanks to A.A., but I think there are a lot of other people in our church who are addicted to alcohol or drugs — people who are ashamed to own the problem, ashamed within their own church to admit being addicted. Isn't our church a family where we can be honest about these things, where we don't have to pretend?"

"Sure, it is, Carolyn," I told her. "Would you be willing to tell your story to your church family?" Carolyn was terrified.

But one Sunday morning she took what we called at that church the "Witness Stand" — a time in worship in which an individual talked briefly about his or her walk with God. Carolyn was wobbly, weak, uncertain, but she told her story. People were deeply moved. They loved and applauded her.

In response to her message, a group of recovering alcoholics and drug addicts came together under Carolyn's leadership to start a ministry called Faith, Hope, and Recovery. At the start, she felt scared and inadequate, but as she began to minister, she found power.

It's scary to step out in ministry when we feel inadequate. Most of us would rather wait around for the Holy Spirit to fill us with power before we risk anything. But Jesus indicates we need to go in obedience and believe that when we get to that needy place, his Spirit will be there. We won't get the power before we go.

I tell those men and women praying about a decision, "If God hasn't made his will clear, choose the scarier option. See if God hasn't already gone before you to prepare the way."

Giving Up Control

A final principle points back to me as pastor.

When I speak to church leaders at workshops and mention how I encourage the formation of dozens and dozens, if not hundreds, of small groups in a church, I am often asked, "Who controls these groups?"

"I hope the Holy Spirit does," I say, "because pastors and church leaders sure can't control all those people."

"But if you turn loose the control of those groups," some ask, "won't unfortunate things happen? Won't it lead to immorality or unsound theology?"

"Well, that's a possibility," I say. "And I think I'm prepared to deal with that. But, in years of doing this type of ministry, as far as I know, no one has been seduced; no heresies have cropped up. Instead, a lot of life-changing ministry has occurred."

As a pastor, I have to trust lay people with ministry if I'm going to see results. I have to put my reputation, and the church's reputation, on the line. As much as I might like to, I can't stand on the bank of the Jordan River and say, "Stop the water." No, like the Israelites crossing to claim the Promised Land, I've got to step in *before* the water recedes.

As I planned one Easter service, I asked a housewife and mother in the congregation to tell her story. "In the morning service, we're going to hear the anthem 'I Know That My Redeemer Lives'," I said. "Would you tell your church family how you know your Redeemer lives?"

On Easter Sunday morning, Jan told her story: "Six years ago I discovered I had cancer. And through my cancer I discovered something else — that I'm a manipulative, controlling woman. I didn't know that before. I discovered that I'm a wife who loves to control my husband, a mom who loves to control my kids. I was made weak. I had to give up control. Today I'm a different person."

Jan could have told how she was healed from cancer, because her cancer was cured. But her witness only incidentally touched on her physical cure. Instead she focused on the more significant change: "In my illness I learned things about myself that I needed to know. My character was sinfully manipulative, and God has changed that, and I thank him."

Jan came to realize that the essence of sin is control, manipulation. The first temptation was, "You shall be like God. You'll be in charge." We all want to run things: our spouses, our children, our businesses. And, yes, we pastors want to run our churches. To put Jesus at the center and let him be in control — that's a radical departure.

And yet, if we don't release lay ministry from the control of the pastor and the staff, we end up with programs so small that a few people can run the whole thing. We miss the life-giving power of God, especially that which comes through lay people sharing in the ministry of pastoral care.

Helping lay people to minister is our call as church leaders. It's an adventuresome undertaking. It means we've got to model vulnerability and limit our requirements for ministry to the bare essentials. Most of all, we've got to give up control and turn them loose.

It's risky. But the alternative is stunted spirituality and diminished pastoral care. Let's take the risk.

*Giving proper pastoral care to people means helping
them become independent in faith in a healthy way.*
— Paul Anderson

CHAPTER TEN

Using the Disciplines to Care

Our youngest child had his first birthday a week after our oldest turned 14. Naturally, our expectations for young Israel differ from those we have for adolescent Andrew. Andrew has moved from total dependence to relative independence. Since he has shown he handles freedom well, he is on his own a fair amount of the time.

Likewise in the church, we have newborn Christians, who are dependent upon the spiritual parents in the church, and mature Christians, who don't require as much regular pastoral direction.

Not that people ever get to the point where they don't need

the personal attention of pastor and church. I know of one Texas pastor who didn't believe his people needed to be visited in the hospital or counseled in times of crisis. All they required was doctrine, he thought, and that alone would enable them to function on their own. That approach fosters an unhealthy independence that only saps a congregation's ability to love and support one another.

Giving proper pastoral care to people means helping them become independent in faith in a healthy way. In a crisis, we are there for them. When they simply want to share what's going on in their lives, we're there. But maturity means they will increasingly take responsibility for their own spiritual growth.

I've found teaching my people spiritual disciplines is one way I can perform this vital form of pastoral care. When people learn to pray, study the Scriptures, tithe, and nurture their own relationship with the Lord, they become increasingly mature. Here, then, are some things we are doing to give this form of pastoral care.

Initial Obstacles

Even though practicing the spiritual disciplines has been for centuries the means of Christian maturity, people often balk when we mention the subject. Before much progress can be made, then, I have to deal, in my preaching and teaching, with a number of objections and obstacles to practicing spiritual disciplines.

1. Disciplines are only for the spiritually elite. In my experience, most Christians wish they were more disciplined. They know they should pray more consistently, read their Bibles more regularly, exercise more faithfully, and spend their time more wisely.

Yet when they don't, and when they also see people they admire who do, seemingly with ease, they become discouraged: "I'm just not a disciplined person," they sigh. After a while they become tired of feeling guilty over what they think they can't accomplish, so they learn to turn off sermon admonitions they believe apply not to them but only to a few choice Christians.

To counter that temptation, we talk about the disciplines as a normal part of the believer's life, not an add-on for the spiritually elite. In the Sermon on the Mount, Jesus spoke about prayer, fasting, and giving as if he expected all people to practice them. So do we.

So, besides mentioning them regularly in the sermons, we introduce spiritual disciplines in the new members class, as part of what it means to be a regular member of the church. We let people know we don't have one set of principles for normal folk and another for all-stars.

2. *Disciplines are a help for ages past but not for years to come.* Unfortunately, many people associate spiritual disciplines with medieval monasteries, monks, and spiritual giants of the past. Perhaps they've heard too many sermon illustrations about Martin Luther and John Wesley getting up early each day for an hour of prayer. As a woman who responded to an article I wrote on fasting put it, "You don't really believe we're supposed to do that in the twentieth century, do you?"

Convincing people of the continued timeliness of spiritual disciplines begins with using illustrations of twentieth century men and women, like Dietrich Bonhoeffer and Corrie ten Boom, who practiced them. But especially important is letting people hear, in worship or small groups, the testimonies of fellow church members who find the disciplines a very present help.

3. *What, me worry?* Then there are those who fear the rise of legalism, which, at first glance, the disciplines can resemble. These people don't want to pervert the grace of God with a "works righteousness," so they are content to relax, put their faith on cruise control, and, in the freedom of the Spirit, let God nurture them as he will.

Such people have a point worth considering. We must not give the impression that practicing the disciplines rests upon human effort. It's not as if once saved by grace, we are required to roll up our sleeves and get to work. We who promote the disciplines can give the false notion that salvation is God's work but sanctification ours. Unfortunately, nowhere is legalism more a temptation than here.

Yet, sloth or dependence on cheap grace also tempt us. The key, then, is to strike the balance of Saint Paul. *"Work out your salvation* with fear and trembling," he begins, but he then adds, *"for God is at work within you,* both to will and to work for his good pleasure" (Phil. 2:12).

I often use Paul's analogy of putting on clothes to explain this creative paradox. God provides us with the clothes of Christ's righteousness. We are saved as we put on Christ. And we grow in Christ the same way we receive Christ, by putting on what is provided for us.

Growing in prayer, for example, is not a matter of perfecting a new practice as much as it is of receiving prayer as a gift of Jesus.

Our part in the process is vital but small compared to God's. He manufactures the clothes; we wear them (although admittedly that often isn't easy). To wear them means to believe they are provided by God and to take and use them as Christ intends.

I've found such teaching avoids the extremes of being "nervous in the service" and practicing "fatalism faith."

4. Dull, dull, dull. Some people imagine that practicing the disciplines regularly will bind them to a dull routine. They think such routine will make their Christian lives stale and thwart their spontaneity and creativity.

I like the way the principal of our Christian school, a woman who models in her family and church the value of the disciplines, responds to this attitude. She says her spiritual routine makes her "stable, not stale." She also points out that ritual need not become "rutual."

As a mother and teacher, she has long observed the power of routine in people's lives. It takes pressure off the mind. Such order, in fact, allows us to be creative. Just as a world that followed natural laws arbitrarily would be impossible to live in, so is an arbitrary life.

Furthermore, successful people establish disciplines that become routine. Magic Johnson of the Los Angeles Lakers threads passes to teammates with precision and beauty. It looks automatic and appears easy. It is, in fact, disciplined brilliance.

My 1-year-old's eating is spontaneous; it is also messy. What has become routine for an adult is, in fact, more enjoyable, since more food lands in the mouth!

The old saying applies to the spiritual life: Freedom without form is chaos.

5. *Only bad people are disciplined.* The word *discipline* reminds some of the unpleasant duty of parents and army sergeants of keeping the unruly in line. Nobody likes to be disciplined. In a country founded and nurtured on the word *freedom*, *discipline* sounds like a dirty word.

Consequently, one needs an attractive carrot to convince this generation, even the Christian sector, that its priorities should include spiritual disciplines. For us the attraction is changed lives.

A woman who has been walking with the Lord for over twenty-five years says that daily time with the Lord has helped her become more willing to pray for extended periods when she seeks God's leading for some special need.

A man enslaved to sexual appetites found that the routine of Bible reading began healing his mind, transformed his self-image from that of a dirty man to a Christian disciple, and released him from the prison of lustful thoughts.

Those who move from the duty to the beauty of discipline are our best advertisements for the value of that seemingly unpleasant word.

Add Training to Teaching

There is a difference between teaching and training. Teaching communicates the material, but training makes sure that it gets into the heart and the hand. Teaching alone will not build disciples. Add training, and you've got a potent combination.

A young man in our church asked if I would perform his wedding ceremony. When I met with him and his fiancée, I had reservations about his readiness for marriage. But I also told him that I would do whatever I could to help him be ready. So I lined him up with two mature men in our congregation. Four months later, we are seeing signs of growth in him. For example, he was more supportive and understanding of his fiancée when she went through struggles. We are more confident now that he will be ready for marriage.

A class alone would not have helped this young man. In fact, he had gone through my Foundations of Faith class and was attending an excellent Sunday school class on communication in marriage. But he needed one-on-one attention. *He* needed the training as much as the teaching.

Training usually requires one-on-one attention. I was encouraged as an assistant pastor to have such a relationship with the senior pastor. We met regularly for prayer and personal counseling. That attention not only shaped my ministry, it also shaped my life.

Training also can happen in small groups. So, the leaders in our church each meet regularly in small groups with members of the congregation. I, for example, meet with a group of four men. We leaders don't want our groups to become more dependent upon us, but upon the Lord. We meet with these people because we and they desire the kind of accountability that can help them walk with the Lord. The agenda for the meetings, in fact, is usually set more by those wanting to be discipled than those doing the discipling.

Naturally, such ministry could more than fill a pastor's schedule. So we've tried to encourage lay people, especially the mature in Christ, to develop their gifts for training people in this way.

About forty of our members are involved in regular one-on-one relationships. They've been trained to speak graciously and regularly with another about specific challenges of the Christian life. They ask such questions as: "How is your devotional time?" "How are things with you and your spouse?" "Where do you struggle to obey the Lord?" In an encouraging way, they prod the person toward greater faithfulness.

One woman was wrestling with a weight problem and wondered how I could help her. After meeting with her once to deal with her bitterness, which lay underneath her weight problem, I asked her to pray for a spiritual counselor from the congregation who could help her. After she recommended someone, I called that person to see if she was willing. She received it as if she had been waiting for the assignment. That was six months ago. They still meet regularly, and the encouragement is flowing in both directions.

Where Two or Three Are Gathered

We also encourage people to meet in home groups to learn and practice the spiritual disciplines corporately.

In a disciplined and orderly way, people go through books of the Bible together in these home groups. Many people have been drawn into consistent Bible reading through this practice. Last year, for example, we read through the Bible together as a congregation.

Following the study, members pray for one another. It is here that some learn to pray with others for the first time. Members have told me, "I never prayed out loud until I got into a home group. Then it seemed more natural."

So, participation in small groups, discussed more thoroughly elsewhere in this book, is an important dimension to teaching the spiritual disciplines.

The Importance of Modeling

Last year, George, a teacher in our congregation, and I roomed together at a leadership conference. As I normally do, each day I rose early for Bible study and prayer.

Later, at one of our congregational retreats, George said this: "When I saw the pastor sneak out early each morning, even after a late evening, I began thinking, *Maybe the Lord would have me do that.* I've regularly spent time in prayer for some time, but seeing his example challenged me to do more. I now give my first hour of the day to the Lord."

George had heard dozens of sermons on prayer, in which I had invited people to get up early to pray. But it was my example that gave impact to the teachings.

Jesus modeled prayer before he taught it. After the disciples observed his life of prayer, they asked, "Lord, teach us to pray, as John taught his disciples." When a leader walks in Christ, it will be easier for his or her people to do so as well.

Consequently, we've encouraged the leaders of our congregation to set a standard in their Christian life for others to follow. It makes a difference. A former member of our congregation, now a pastor, said that when he was a member, knowing the leaders were giving quality and quantity time to prayer made him want to do the same. One of our young fathers recently said, "As I saw the leadership applying various disciplines to their lives, I wanted to grow in Christ along with them."

Wings to Fly

The oldest of my five children, Andrew, is a big help around the house. He is more mechanically minded than I am and is learning to be a good fix-it man. He is also a good running partner. We'd like to do a marathon together some day.

When it's time for Andrew to leave the nest, there is one papa bird that will have mixed emotions. But seeing how the Lord is causing him to mature, I am confident that God has exciting things in store for him — even if I can't watch at close range.

As a pastor, I sometimes struggle to release my people into their God-ordained callings. My messiah complex is one of the things that drove me into the ministry in the first place! Yet part of pastoral care, I've discovered, is to overcome the temptation to keep people in my nest eternally, to let God, by means of the spiritual disciplines, give them wings to fly on their own.

A priest is a channel of forgiveness, grace, mercy, healing. A priest provides pastoral care. This is what God has called every believer to do and to be. The first step, then, in helping people move into ministry is to remind them of that, to tell them, "You are priests."

— Bruce Larson

CHAPTER ELEVEN

Helping People Care for One Another

Over a decade ago, I visited an exciting church in the inner city of Chicago. While most Sunday sermons in that neighborhood echoed through half-empty auditoriums, the sermons of this church's pastor reached overflow crowds Sunday after Sunday. Obviously, it was an unusual church. People weren't just dropping their money in the plate and then putting their feet up while the pastor did all the work. They believed they were called to minister and by God's power *could* minister.

I had a chance to talk at length with the pastor. "What's the secret of your success here?"

"Simple," he said. "I just tell people who they are — chosen by God, his children, his priests. I don't shame them for what they are not; I tell them who they are."

At that moment, I promised myself, *If ever I return to the pastorate, I'm going to remember that.* I did return, and I kept that promise. I've been telling people who they are, and it works. As I am just getting my feet wet in my new position at the Crystal Cathedral, let me use my experience with University Presbyterian Church's (UPC) lay ministry as a prime example.

A Kingdom of Priests

Just before God gave Moses the Law, he instructed Moses to tell the people they were to be a kingdom of priests (Exod. 19:6). The New Testament repeats that theme. Peter refers to the believers as a holy and royal priesthood (1 Pet. 2:5, 9). At the very end of the Bible, the same theme is repeated, that Christians are called to be a kingdom of priests (Rev. 1:6).

Primarily, a priest is a person who mediates between God and another person. A priest is a channel of forgiveness, grace, mercy, healing. A priest provides pastoral care. This is what God has called every believer to do and to be. The first step, then, in helping people move into ministry is to remind them of that, to tell them, "You are priests."

For the most part, Jesus didn't pick as his disciples the highly trained, the well educated. Not that he chose unqualified people; I think those twelve were the *most* qualified. They didn't have to unlearn other disciplines. They had clean slates. At least three were fishermen, and one was a government employee, but none were clergy (rabbis).

These are the men told by Jesus, "I will make you fishers of men." He didn't say, "Maybe you will be" or "I'll try to teach you how." He said they would become that, and they did.

But what does that mean today — to be fishers of men, to be priests? When we tell people they are priests, what are we calling them to do?

I believe this priesthood involves four facets of ministry, four separate roles in which every Christian needs to function. We all are to be evangelists, ministers of healing, missionaries, and prophets.

Called to Be Evangelists

When I arrived at UPC, the evangelism department had just two responsibilities: to provide a special evangelistic speaker for one week each year and to follow up on visitors.

I left the structure alone for a year so I could evaluate the program's weaknesses and strengths. After that, I proposed to the Session, "How about dropping the evangelism department? Every member of this church is called to be an evangelist, to talk about Jesus to the people where we live and work. Having a department responsible for this lets us off the hook. Let's make evangelism everybody's job."

That challenge needed some explaining, of course. We had to help our congregation understand that evangelists aren't scholars who teach theology, though occasionally they are. An evangelist is an introducer. Not everyone can teach; anybody can introduce.

An evangelist merely says to someone experiencing the pain of life, "Have you had enough? I want you to meet the ultimate Someone who can change your life — Jesus Christ."

In eight years with no evangelism program, that congregation nearly doubled. We received about four hundred new members each year. The believers were the evangelists, and they were taking that commission seriously.

Called to Be Ministers of Healing

While evangelism is a ministry to the nonbeliever, the ministry of healing most often takes place between believers. We are priests, called into each others' lives to be agents of all kinds of healing — emotional, relational, physical, mental, vocational.

At UPC, we provided one setting for that to take place — a quarterly healing service. Anyone who wanted could come forward for prayer with the pastors and elders. But the primary setting for this ministry was the small group.

The Christian community provides a powerful healing climate. When "two or three are gathered," the Holy Spirit's power is made manifest, just as Jesus promised. In that climate of love, one person may reveal a problem and the others listen and pray, and healing takes place. Openness and honesty, walking in the light — all are powerful medicines.

Healing is not the province of the specialized few; a secular study some years ago proved that. It was done to determine which school of counseling — Rogerian, Freudian, Jungian, and so on — produced the best results. The results were intriguing. The most effective counseling was provided not by the disciples of any of these professional schools, but by the control groups used in the study. Ordinary people — airline pilots, secretaries, housewives, businesspersons — with no therapy training, who simply spent time listening, produced better results than the professionals.

It has been said that only about one person in ten seeking counseling has special needs requiring professional help. The other 90 percent are well served by talking to a sympathetic lay person. For instance, early in this century, there was no cure for alcoholism. It was not until two untrained laymen discovered the Twelve Steps of Alcoholics Anonymous that there was any concrete program for recovery.

UPC offered dozens of groups for people with special problems. There were groups for the addicted, for cancer patients, for the unemployed, for stroke victims, for the divorced, for single parents. The healing ministry was largely in the hands of unpaid lay people, but they were people filled with God's love and the healing power of his Holy Spirit.

We did, of course, refer extreme cases to a counseling service, but we avoided adding a professional counselor to the church staff. Had we done that, we felt, we would have sent the wrong message to our church family. Instead, we said, both by word and action, "You are ministers of healing."

Called to Be Missionaries

The Jesus who said, "Come unto me, all ye who are heavy laden" also said, "Go ye into all the world." Our call to discipleship includes the command to *go*. We are sent forth in mission.

On Sunday mornings at UPC, our worship service included a commissioning of those who were *going* as missionaries, both at home and abroad. One year, 356 people served overseas. A few were long-term career missionaries. Others went for a year to teach English in China. Many took "a vacation with a purpose," working two weeks or more at an orphanage in Baja California or roofing buildings in Jamaica. These efforts were directed by our able pastor of world missions, Arthur Beals, a gifted man whose contacts all over the world helped the church connect people eager to serve with appropriate overseas opportunities.

To prepare people for cross-cultural ministry, UPC's Christian education curriculum included a class on being a world Christian. But actually, the bulk of this kind of training was not done in the classroom. Would-be missionaries were called on to practice cross-cultural missions right there in Seattle.

UPC was located just one block from the main drag of the University District. Any time of the day or night, within a two- or three-block stretch, you could find almost any ethnic group: Aleuts and Eskimos, Latins and Europeans, Africans and Asians. Mixed in were gang members, students, drug pushers, professors, punkers, shoppers, winos, and bag ladies. Adopting Jesus' own method, people went out to that area in groups of two or three to meet some of those people from other cultures and find ways to minister to them.

Three of our young singles were walking in the University District, practicing cross-cultural mission in preparation for a mission trip to Mexico. A young man sitting on the curb asked them for money. They sat down with him. He was smelly, dirty, and unshaven but pleasant and friendly.

"Why do you need money?" they asked.

"I can't get a job."

"Do you want one?"

"Oh, yeah, I want a job. I'll do anything."

While one of the group sat with him, the other two covered both sides of the street, going into every store to ask if it was hiring.

They discovered that a nearby pizza restaurant needed a dishwasher and arranged an interview for 1:00 the next day. The three took the young man home, got him some presentable clothes, and gave him a place to bathe and shave.

He showed up at the restaurant the next day at twelve — an hour early — and got the job. And he kept the job. Later, he started coming to church and eventually became a Christian.

Our church family found you don't have to go overseas to do missionary work. You can become a missionary wherever you find people.

Several years back, some UPC members began helping out a few Southeast Asian refugees — providing clothes for them, finding some basic furniture for their new homes. From that modest beginning, the church saw the emergence of what became the largest Cambodian church outside of Cambodia. That church was the flowering of missionary work done in Seattle by some Christians who cared.

Mission can begin across the street as well as across the world, and it's not confined to a few well-trained career missionaries. The UPC church family experienced that reality.

Called to Be Prophets

This priesthood to which we're called involves a fourth role: prophet. A prophet is not primarily a *fore*teller (a future-teller) but a *forth*teller, one who speaks forth for God about the social evils of the time. "People are being oppressed," the prophet says. "Injustice and immorality are rampant. God has a better way if we will serve him and be obedient."

In earlier centuries, the church was on the cutting edge of social change — establishing orphanages, hospitals, schools, programs for the poor. Today, all too often, we end up sweeping up behind the parade, tagging along after the courageous efforts of others.

It doesn't need to be that way. The church can and should be producing the people who are leading us into a more peaceful, benevolent, and just society.

One member at UPC was the Seattle superintendent of schools, and I saw him in this kind of prophetic role. When he arrived a few years back, Bill Kendrick inherited an almost hopeless situation — 43,000 students with a diminishing financial base and a growing number of impoverished students. Hundreds of families had already put their children in private schools or moved out of the school district.

Bill was realistic about the problems, but he also noticed that some students were succeeding in spite of those problems. Most of those children came from Asian cultures — Cambodian, Chinese, Vietnamese — where education was a top priority. They had parents with high expectations who told their kids, "You will not play hooky. You will do your homework. You will bring home A's." And they did.

Bill saw the need for that kind of role model for all the kids. So whenever he spoke to Kiwanis Club, Lions, or Rotary, he shared his vision to find an ombudsman, an encourager, for every student in the Seattle schools, one person outside the school system who would care for that kid and hold him or her accountable.

All kinds of people responded: chief executive officers, lawyers, businesspeople, accountants. Each one — over twenty thousand at one count — was linked with a student.

All that was the result of one man's efforts to change the climate and increase the potential for excellence in the public schools. There's a better way to do what's being done in every area of life. There's a better way to practice medicine and law, to conduct business and social services, to do police work and education.

In our jobs, in PTA or the Garden Club, and even in our churches, there's a better way to do whatever is being done. The Holy Spirit is the author of creativity, and we can tap into that creativity.

Prophets, Old Testament or twentieth century, are those men and women who are called to make a difference, and that prophetic role is an essential element of the holy priesthood we Christians are called to.

The sanctuary of University Presbyterian Church was no larger than those of nearby congregations. Remarkably, however, ours was so filled three times each Sunday morning that it took three traffic officers to direct cars in and out of the parking lot.

But that Sunday morning turnout, encouraging as it was, couldn't measure the impact of the kingdom of priests unleashed over Seattle during the remaining six days of the week. In homes, schools, factories, and offices, they deployed — as evangelists, ministers, missionaries, and prophets. They were performing pastoral care, both for one another and for a world that needed their ministration.

If we aren't making a difference beyond our walls, are we the church? But if we are making a difference, there's going to be battle fatigue.

— Paul Anderson

CHAPTER TWELVE
Balancing Service and Solace

A few years ago, our church began to catch the vision: Christ our Lord was sending us out to be his agents in the fight against evil, suffering, and brokenness.

That was about the time churches in our community began to take more seriously our responsibility to the local needy. We started small, first opening a simple food pantry at one church, offering food once a week. Eventually sixteen churches were offering help several times a week.

We also "converted" a bar so that we could feed and minister to the homeless, destitute, and street people. Next a home was opened to disciple men who became Christians and wanted their lives changed. A women's home is now in the planning stage.

Our church became acquainted with the staffs at the local Alcohol Recovery Center and Eating Disorders Clinic. We were eventually asked to start a chaplaincy program at the hospital, as well as a Sunday morning worship service.

In addition, a twelve-step group was established at our church to help recovering alcoholics strengthen their roots in Christ. Another group worked with the sexually abused.

We continue to look for other ways to advance the gospel beyond the church walls.

We'd realized anew that Jesus does not want us to minister just to transplanted Lutherans but also to the poor and lost. So, pastoral care mainly meant getting people ready for battle. Our church was first and foremost an army barracks, from which members go out, march against the forces of evil, and establish outposts for the kingdom in enemy territory.

This concept is certainly justified by Scripture, from Jesus' strong words "Go, therefore . . ." to the eloquent model of Paul's ministry. But it took me awhile before I discovered that pastoral care was bigger than rushing people through basic training and sending them off to war.

War Makes for Heroes

Not that the church as army barracks has nothing to offer the church. There are many practical advantages to emphasizing this aspect of pastoral care.

● *People are drawn into action.* Recently I asked the man who heads our ministry called "The Crossing" what experience he had to equip him for work with street people. He answered, "None; just availability." He also encourages others to make themselves available to God and then see what happens.

This man recognizes the spiritual battle going on. He's not going to wait around until he gets training for every contingency.

He doesn't want to squander a minute, so even if he's not fully prepared, he's willing to do something. When people see the church engaged in spiritual warfare, they are more willing to be drawn into ministry outside the church.

● *People squabble less about nonessentials.* Soldiers complain about their food when they are in training. On the front lines, where far more critical issues are at stake, it's no big deal if you find an ant in your stew.

The church that isn't dealing with life-and-death matters eventually squabbles about relatively insignificant things — like what color to paint the kitchen or which room to let the Boy Scout troop use. When a church is engaged in front-line ministries, people are less concerned about niceties on the home front.

● *People are more willing to sacrifice.* Just as soldiers on the front lines often build up a high tolerance for pain and more willingly perform the heroic act, so are front-line Christians more willing to sacrifice for their Lord and one another.

Because of his concern for needy people and his love for God, Ed has poured himself into a ministry with the poor in our community. In the morning, before going to his job, he often stops at the church to attend to some matter of this ministry. After work he sometimes goes straight to church, often working for three hours or so.

Once I expressed to his wife my concern that Ed might exhaust himself. She replied, "Nobody will burn out Ed." And it's true; he's been going at it like this for years now.

It is clear to me, then, that my pastoral-care ministry includes deploying the church "militant."

Battle Fatigue

For a while our army barracks contained no infirmary. We sought to be sensitive to needy people, but we were not aware of how much some of our soldiers were hurting.

A young man gifted in finances took over our bookkeeping and joined the church council. John spent countless hours cleaning up our books and helping establish better financial policies.

Everyone appreciated his work, except John's wife. John had been spending so much time at church, his family life began to suffer. His wife particularly resented his being away from the home so much. Finally, she said she had had enough, and John's involvement came to a screeching halt.

Things are better now. His wife, in fact is more involved than John these days. But for a time, they were a wounded family.

I recently learned a song, "I am a wounded soldier, but I will not leave the fight." I like the song, but I fear for the corporal who badly needs treatment yet keeps on fighting. We had more of that kind than I cared to realize.

And I was one of them. Over the years I began to notice that some of my dreams of spiritual victories had to yield to hard reality. I have been tempered by personal defeat (I am not getting holy as fast as I planned to), by family loss (two believing sisters were divorced by their husbands, one a minister, altogether involving seven children), by unanswered prayers (my father died of cancer despite the fervent prayers of many, and our fourth child died shortly before birth in spite of our confidence that "this birth is going to be easier").

I love the ministry, but it's a lot harder than I previously thought. I still talk about victory and glory. But I talk more about the Cross, more about suffering for Christ's sake. I'm still a fighter, but I've come to see that the church must be more than an army barracks, where soldiers are trained to go out from victory to victory. It's also an infirmary, a hospital where those bruised in battle and battered by life can receive the healing touch of the Great Physician.

Pastoral care must emphasize both aspects, and that meant opening up an infirmary.

Hospital Benefits

Besides comforting and consoling people, viewing the church as a hospital for hurting persons has other benefits.

- *People more readily admit their neediness.* A few years ago, I would not have told the congregation that I sometimes fight with my wife and seriously struggle in my faith. My reasoning probably went something like this: "If they are to imitate me as I imitate Christ, then I had better be careful what they're imitating."

People, however, could not identify with me or my wife because we were thought to have a model marriage, a together family, and an ever victorious Christian life. The guy in the pew who was struggling with pornography could not brave coming to the pastor when he kept hearing about the call to holiness. He was sure that the leadership didn't ever battle with such problems.

However, when I was finally willing to embrace the idea that the church is a hospital for sinners, including me, and talk honestly about my Christian walk in my preaching, teaching, and counseling, my people opened up themselves. As Lisa, a young mother who grew up in the congregation, put it: "We thought that you and the elders had it together. We were afraid to talk about our problems." Now they're talking, and they are getting the help they need.

One young mother said after a counseling session with my wife and me, "A few years ago, people were considered weirdoes if they were getting counseling. No more, thank goodness."

● *People more readily seek help.* For some time we've announced that following each worship service, people can come to the prayer chapel to be prayed for by another. There was a time when no one would show, but that seldom happens anymore. People are realizing they can come for prayer and not be suspected of some serious perversion or problem.

We held a seminar on sexual abuse three years ago. The honesty of David, the speaker, who shared his battles with homosexuality, crime, drugs, sex, and abuse opened the door for others. Longstanding members of the church came forward for prayer, people who never before had told me about their histories in these areas. A support group was formed to help the sexually abused.

Other groups have since formed to address different needs. Some men who are new believers meet weekly to go through a twelve-step program. Some young mothers who get weary of the little ones knocking on their knees meet for mutual support.

● *Preaching can address the tender side of humanity.* How a pastor speaks to his people depends upon how he views them. Are they primarily haughty or hungry?

I used to love it when my father, also a pastor, would scold people on Sundays. I would say to myself, *Give it to them, Dad. They deserve it.* And in my army barracks mentality, I tended toward scolding or bold challenges: "If we take Jesus seriously, we will———. So let's put aside our excuses and go out and do it, as Christ commands!"

But I've discovered that many people respond more readily to a shepherd than a drill sergeant. Besides, I've listened to enough stories from my parishioners and endured sufficient personal trials to understand that sin is both rebellion *and* bondage. Formerly, I assumed the willful disobedience of people when I preached; now I remember that many people want to change but feel they can't. Sometimes it's better to say, "We take Jesus seriously, but still we find it hard to follow. Let Christ take your hand; he'll help you through your struggles and enable you to do what he commands."

Hospitals Can Make People Sick

As healthy as a hospital can be, if it becomes the sole image of the church, it can begin to make people spiritually sick.

● *The war may get put on hold.* I could become a full-time doctor of souls. Needs abound. As soon as I meet one crisis, three more surface on the other side of town.

We are grateful for our ministry to people recovering from chemical abuse. Yet these people, who sometimes remain unstable as they recover, can live from one crisis to the next. When they are evicted from their apartments, they need counseling and then help finding new apartments and moving. When family tensions erupt, as they inevitably will during recovery, people need intervention. I can easily put in three days dealing with a series of crises like this, and afterwards, I'm hardly ready to prepare a sermon or preach.

We've learned to link such people with caring members of the church. That helps, but the fact remains: the infirmary never empties. Pastors can become so taken up with running a clinic that they never get out to lead their people into new battles.

• *Front-line fighters may feel ignored.* People who reach out to the homeless or alcoholics or the lost, who are on the front lines of ministry, may lose their will to fight and sacrifice if they feel the church is primarily interested in those who show up in worship.

"The pastor now has more time for them than he does for us," one front-line soldier in my congregation said to her friend one day. Naturally, people on the front also need the pastor's oversight and the congregation's affirmation to keep them going.

• *A hospital can become a cozy place.* It's a lot easier to have three meals a day served to you in bed than to trudge through the jungle in army boots. Sick people get sympathy cards and candy. They are forgiven for being irresponsible. Some actually prefer the enema to the enemy.

A former navy officer told me the "purpose of the medical corps is to keep as many men at as many guns for as many days as possible." After care is given, a soldier has stamped on his medical jacket ATC (all treatment complete) or AETC (all essential treatment complete). AETC means a soldier can be put back into action even if not fully recovered. Then, if there is a lull in the fighting, he can return for further treatment.

The ultimate purpose of Christian hospital care is to get people fit to fight again. As needy sinners, they'll never be stamped ATC, at least until the *parousia*. But AETC is good enough to reenter the ranks for Christ in this life.

• *Care can become faddish.* With so many seeking counseling, some people actually wonder if something is wrong if they don't have something to talk to a psychologist about. Yet most people don't need constant hospital care. Sure they get discouraged or resentful or listless. But they probably don't need therapy; they need simply to pray more fervently or forgive more readily or get out of their easy chairs more often.

How many wars would an army win if 50 percent of their troops were in the infirmary? We must bring our people the healing that comes from the Cross and then help them walk in health, so they can fight as soldiers of Jesus Christ.

Both the Barracks and the Bedside

So for our church it must be both — hospital *and* army barracks. If we aren't making a difference beyond our walls, are we the church? But if we are making a difference, there will be battle fatigue. If we aren't sensitive to both, soon we'll be fighting each other instead of the enemy.

The good news is that it is not impossible to emphasize both. Some of our best soldiers, in fact, are those who are most recently out of the infirmary. And some soldiers find that visiting the hospital makes them better soldiers.

No one has brought more people to church in the last year than Kathy and Oli. These two women have plenty of friends in the AA group they attend, and one by one they bring them in. For example, Oli worked with a Native American woman who had attempted suicide, was desperately trying to survive, but who also had begun recovering from alcoholic abuse.

At the same time, Oli and Kathy know they are far from whole. They lose occasional battles and need encouragement to carry on. So they return to us regularly on an "outpatient" basis. They receive counseling and participate in support groups.

Oli and Kathy show me that it is not only desirable but possible to keep my pastoral care moving back and forth between the bedside and the battlefield.

Doug, a businessman friend in my congregation, told me he envied what I got to do hour by hour, day by day: care for people's spiritual welfare.

— *Mark Galli*

Epilogue

In one of my periodic fits to get fit, I took up running. Another time I took up swimming. Another time still I took up biking. But I was never happy.

When I ran, my arms remained flabby. When I swam, my running suffered. When I biked (at my usual leisurely pace), my lung capacity shrank.

Then one day at a running race, I met Ingrid the athlete. She trained for triathlons. Each day she ran, swam, *and* biked. It took her between six and eight hours, but each day she did it. I was impressed. I envied her. I hated her.

Then again, I was surprised to learn that many people are impressed by pastors. A few years ago, Doug, a businessman friend in my congregation, told me he envied what I got to do hour by hour, day by day: care for people's spiritual welfare. And if he would have known the variety of pastoral care pastors get to practice, he would have hated me.

That variety has been manifested in this book. To encourage lay people to care for one another and reach out to the world is one aspect of pastoral care. To prompt people to go deeper in the Spirit is another. To engage people in their homes and on the job is another still.

Ignoring two in the pursuit of one would leave pastors with nagging concerns about what ministry isn't getting done. But pastors don't have to choose between them. All three are part of most pastors' routine. You could call it the triathlon of pastoral care.

However, there's something different about this triathlon. In the first place, in pastoral care we pursue a more noble goal than getting ourselves into physical shape; instead, we give our days to help others get into spiritual shape. And second, although pastoral care can be tiring at times, there are few activities more invigorating than speaking of things eternal with people, one by one. It's difficult to imagine a higher calling in life.

So, Ingrid, take that.